THE *Successful* HEALTH PRACTITIONER

The 5 +1 Non-Negotiable Pillars
to Grow Your Online Business,
Get Clients, & Ditch Your Day Job

Lori Kennedy

Copyright © Lori Kennedy, Inc., 2019

All rights reserved. No part of this book may be reproduced in any form without permission in writing from the author. Reviewers may quote brief passages in reviews.

Published 2020

DISCLAIMER

No part of this publication may be reproduced or transmitted in any form or by any means, mechanical or electronic, including photocopying or recording, or by any information storage and retrieval system now known or hereafter invented, or transmitted by email without permission in writing from the author.

Neither the author nor the publisher assumes any responsibility for errors, omissions, or contrary interpretations of the subject matter herein. Any perceived slight of any individual or organization is purely unintentional.

Brand and product names are trademarks or registered trademarks of their respective owners.

I dedicate this book to my community.
There would be no book without you.
We're in this together.

#INSPIREDHUSTLE

TABLE OF CONTENTS

INTRODUCTION.. 1

Chapter 1:
WHY I COULDN'T GET CLIENTS & MAKE MONEY............................. 7

Chapter 2:
HOW ALMOST GETTING FIRED SAVED MY BUSINESS 15

Chapter 3:
THE MODEL THAT GAVE ME A MULTIMILLION DOLLAR BUSINESS.... 25

Chapter 4:
LAY A SOLID FOUNDATION TO GROW FROM..................................... 48

Chapter 5:
PILLAR +1: WHO DO YOU WANT TO SERVE?
(NAIL THIS OR RISK FAILING) 62

Chapter 6:
PILLAR 1: HOW TO STAND OUT FROM THE CROWD 77

Chapter 7:
PILLAR 2: THE KLT + E SEQUENCE... 99

Chapter 8:
PILLAR 3: GETTING THE YES! 109

Chapter 9:
PILLAR 4: BUILD THE METHODOLOGY
(THE SIGNATURE PROGRAM) 154

Chapter 10:
PILLAR 5: KEEP CLIENTS FOR LIFE 210

Chapter 11:
WILL THIS WORK FOR ME? 216

Chapter 12:
THE BUSINESS AND LIFE OF YOUR DREAMS.................................... 225

ACKNOWLEDGMENTS.. 230

ABOUT THE AUTHOR 232

A RESOURCE YOU WANT & NEED 233

INTRODUCTION

"How's your business going?"

"Um, good. I'm really loving it."

I used to dread that question. Do I lie? Or do I share the truth about what's really going on? It wasn't too long ago that the question used to bring me to my knees. It doesn't anymore. It took me two long and painful years to figure out how to grow my nutrition business in a way that supported the kind of life that I wanted.

That's why I am so glad (and relieved) that you're here.

I wrote this book because it is the one that I would have wanted to read back in 2008/2009 when the only thing running through my mind was, "How am I going to make this work?"

In this book, I'm giving you two things. The second is more important than the first.

The first thing you'll get are the exact steps that I took so that I could get the people that I most wanted to work with to know that I existed and how I turned my failing 1:1 practice into a six-figure program. I will walk you through the 5 +1 Pillars that make up my Health Expert Business Model and give you the simple steps to take so that you can just copy what I did without having to waste time reinventing the wheel.

I'm giving you the framework to turn your 'expensive hobby' into a legit, money-making business so that you can feel proud that you're helping clients and bringing home the bacon (sorry vegans).

The second thing you'll get in this book is, in my opinion, more important than the first. It's this second thing that will determine whether or not you end up getting clients and ditching your day job: *self-belief*.

I can give you strategies all day long. In fact, I've got 20 years of tactics and strategies. But it will always feel like you're working without gain unless you acknowledge this one truth: the only thing that is standing in your way and stopping you from growing your business, getting clients, and being able to ditch your day job is *fear*.

I've had the honor to work with thousands of practitioners and coaches over the last decade and mentor them successfully through the exact same process I'm giving you in this book. That's how I know with full confidence that, ultimately, it's going to be Fear (or the lack of self-belief) that will hold you back—not the fact that you don't have a pretty logo, or that your Facebook group isn't engaged, or that your mother-in-law makes passive-aggressive comments to you every Thanksgiving.

I'm going to reveal lots of personal, difficult-to-tell stories and share with you my most vulnerable experiences so that you will know that you are not alone and that you can confidently build your business. In addition to that, I am giving you the steps and specific instructions on what to do. Whether you actually take those steps comes down to your willingness to take action despite feeling the fear.

It's important to understand that starting from zero—zero idea what you're doing, zero client experience, zero skills, zero people on your email list, zero social media following, zero sales, zero (or less than zero if you've got student debt) dollars made—is where *everyone* starts. If you want to do something you've never done before (like growing a business on the internet, *ahem*), then it's important to acknowledge where you are and the fears that you currently believe about yourself and your capability. The self-awareness that comes with this acknowledgment is your most valuable tool.

Why?

Have you ever felt like a fraud? For years the voice in my head was screaming, "Who do you think you are? Don't be too bossy or people will think you're a bitch. Don't be too much, you'll make people feel uncomfortable." Have you ever doubted your ability to make it work? What about worrying that you won't be able to help your clients get results, or that nobody will buy your program? Well you aren't the only one—it's called imposter syndrome.

What is stopping you from gaining momentum and achieving the type of business and success you desire? It's not that you're lacking information, that you're *allergic* to technology and don't know how to use social media effectively, that you don't know what your niche is, that you work a full-time job, that you don't have client experience, or that you're so heavily regulated that your hands are tied. It's that you feel this way and believe these perceived limitations as truths; when in reality, they are not.

They are just things you believe as truths because you were conditioned to think and feel this way, maybe by your family, culture, society, or social media. Sure, we've come a long way, but if you pull back the curtain in most homes, the division of labor is far from equal. Recognizing the fears and limiting beliefs we've come to hold as true about ourselves is key to being able to process through them so that they no longer inhibit the actions that have been proven to produce momentum and the type of success you desire.

This is why I do what I do—to both teach and empower you to become a better version of yourself. That's why I create and publish content, run a community, and host the Business Of Becoming podcast. It's also why I share that I drink Diet Coke and that I would rather not shower. It's why I show up on Instagram Stories in the same shirt three days in a row. It's why I openly share my own struggles and the ways I've worked through them. It's why I talk about what it's like to be highly sensitive, an intuitive empath, a mother, divorced, and a CEO—it's why I share both the light *and* the dark moments.

All the content that I've created over the last decade demonstrates how I'm still learning and growing, and how I'm certainly not perfect. I have no desire to be! And yet—despite all the blogs, the social media posts, and the podcast episodes; despite all the step-by-step instruction, the free training, and the Facebook Lives where I both teach and cry—I still get emails and private messages and see posts from smart, passionate, and purpose-driven practitioners and coaches who are overwhelmed and stuck. These are real people who want so badly to help others, to contribute to their households, to achieve a level of success that would make anyone's head spin, and most importantly, to live up to their full potential.

My responses are always professional and identical. I tell them that everyone starts from scratch, that they most certainly have what it takes, that they are not alone, and that, yes, this is most definitely harder than they thought it would be but that it doesn't have to be. It's a choice.

What I really want to do is to hug them and then get on my soapbox and yell at the top of my lungs, "WTF?! Can't you see that all these feelings and obstacles are being put in front of you on purpose, for your own benefit? If growing a business that has the ability to replace your day job *and* transform people's health was easy, then everyone would do it. But it's not easy, and they're not doing it. It is simple, it's just not easy. So, if you want to take the road less-traveled, grow a business, and ditch your day job, then stop letting fear block your way! Surrender to the journey and know this: you are in control of how it turns out."

Will you be successful overnight? Nope. Will there be light and dark moments? Always, and maybe you'll experience both at the same time. Will ideas and shiny objects distract you? Of course, you're a creative person. If your journey is anything like mine—and it doesn't have to be—you'll also gain 20lb of stress weight and then decide you must deal with your emotional eating issues. Will you want to throw in the towel more than once? I don't know anyone who's built their own business who hasn't fantasized about just walking away and working at Starbucks. But you won't, because in your bones you know that you were meant for more and that the only real way to fail is by quitting.

But you won't have to quit because now you have this book setting out the exact steps to take so you can grow your business; you have me in your corner believing in you super hard and cheering you on like the crazy, screaming hockey mom that I am. More than anything, I hope that this book gives you peace of mind. Know that the steps are all laid out, that they work, and that the only requirement is for you to show up daily and take imperfect action like it's your job. Because it is.

Ready to grow your business, get clients, and ditch your day job?

Let's do it!

With love & inspired hustle,

Lori

Chapter 1

WHY I COULDN'T GET CLIENTS & MAKE MONEY

I had to go to lunch at my parents' house. We were having a family lunch, which meant that my older cousins would be there. They were all professionals with impressive careers, and I knew that one of them would ask the one question I was absolutely dreading.

It had been about six months since I graduated as a registered holistic nutritionist. I had been busily trying to establish myself, but I was nowhere near the level of success that I had anticipated or hoped for. Of course, I had no frame of reference for success; I just assumed I'd be further ahead than I was. As you can imagine, I wasn't looking forward to this lunch. What did I do? I put on my most sophisticated top and mentally prepared myself to go to lunch.

I admired my cousins so much. When I was younger, I remember always wanting to be older so I could take part in their conversations. That's really why I was dreading the lunch so much. At that point in my life, I didn't feel like I had anything to offer—like I had nothing to bring to the table.

As we sat down to eat, I looked at the spread: bagels, cream cheese, tuna, egg salad, and all the condiments you'd typically fill up on at a Sunday brunch. It was bad enough that I already felt like a weirdo since I no longer ate 'normal food'. Yeah, I was that preachy nutritionist who stopped eating gluten and dairy and felt like everyone else should too.

So I started to fill my plate with the tuna and egg and I passed on the bagels, which in my family back then was a sin. Then came the dreaded topic of conversation. Work. I held my breath, hoping that no one would ask me the question…

"Lori, how's your business going?"

Shit. And there it was. Inevitably, they had asked it. Would it be weird if I excused myself to go to the bathroom without answering? Maybe if I spilled my tuna and egg on the floor that would distract everyone long enough for the conversation to change topic. I thought of pretending to choke just so I wouldn't have to answer.

Before arriving at my parents' house, I had mentally gone over all the ways in which I could answer that question without feeling like a total failure. The only solution I had come up with was to lie—because at the time the truth was too embarrassing to share. I didn't want to lose face. I wasn't ready for their pity.

The worst part about the whole situation was that I was trying so hard to succeed with my nutrition practice, but nothing I was doing was working. I sat in my office day in, day out with my very green website, my very green professionally designed logo, perfectly organized forms, and glossy brochures, hoping that the chiropractor who had promised referrals would come through with some.

At that moment, sitting around the table judged by cousins and bagels alike, I felt like I was in the witness box and had just pledged to tell the truth, the whole truth, and nothing but the truth, so help me God.

So I took a deep breath and told the truth. Surprisingly, I didn't burst into tears as I blurted out what was really going on.

"Well, it's not going great. Actually, the whole thing sucks. I'm burning through money. I'm paying rent for an office in a very busy chiropractic office. The chiropractor promised me referrals, but she isn't giving me any. I'm putting up flyers for free talks and no one is coming."

Then my Mom chimed in: "But I came to one and brought Vivian. We both thought your talk was very informative." Um, thanks, Mom.

"I have this website and it's not getting me any clients. I tried to talk to the chiropractor, and she told me to hand out flyers to her patients. But no one is booking sessions with me. I had one client who paid me $150, and then I spent six hours putting together a program for her that she said was too hard to follow."

"It's been six months since I graduated, and I haven't really made any money," I continued. "I feel like I wasted my time going to school because I don't have any clients. So... um, yeah, it's not going great. How's everything with you?"

I think one of my cousins replied with, "Oh, that sucks."

My other cousin asked, "Did you get business training in school?"

"Yeah, we did. I'm doing everything I was taught, but it's not working. I don't know what else to do. I rented a clinic space. I spent money on building a website. I spent so many hours working on free talks and blog posts and putting together client plans, but none of it is working." None of them had ever started their own business so they couldn't really offer me any advice.

While sitting around that table, I realized that I was on my own to figure out how to make my business work. If I wanted to make a real go at this, I would have to find a way to get clients. I left my parents' house feeling embarrassed and exposed. Up to that point, I hadn't told anyone how it was really going for me.

When I was in school, I didn't give any thought to the business side of things. Sure, we had a business course; it was 12 hours long and talked about things like business cards and insurance requirements. I realize times have changed and access to business training is widely available now, but this was 2007. It honestly never occurred to me that I would be starting up and running my own business. CEO, what's that?

In my head, it went like this:

- Go to school
- Study
- Take exams
- Pass exams
- Get letters after your name
- Open up a practice
- Get clients
- Be successful

But that was not my current reality. I felt blindsided. Did I miss the lesson on "you are now a business owner, and here's the guidebook to start your own business"? I should have realized I would be starting my own practice, but for whatever reason, I didn't think of it like that. It was like nobody told me I'd be starting up my own business and what that would entail. I was a registered holistic nutritionist with a passion for helping people get rid of candida—a systemic fungal infection caused by yeast overgrowth. At that point I didn't self-identify as a founder and CEO navigating a startup business.

I stayed at that clinic for three more months trying to make it work. It wasn't until I had a hard conversation with Bryan, my then-husband that I realized I could no longer afford to continue paying the rent for my office. I would have to terminate my clinic rental agreement and go back to personal training at the gym where I had previously been working.

I hated having that conversation, but I knew he was right. There was no justifiable reason for me to continue pursuing something that was clearly failing. But the most frustrating thing about it was that I had no idea why it wasn't working or how to fix it.

So the next day I mustered up my courage and asked the chiropractor if she would please release me early from our one-year rental agreement. She agreed and was very kind about it. I thanked her, packed up all my very professional office paraphernalia, and walked as quickly as I could to the car, biting my lip the whole way. I was determined not to cry until I was safely in the confines of my car.

Then flooded in the tears. Like, ugly crying. I felt so defeated. I felt like a complete loser. I felt like I was moving backward by returning to the gym to work as a personal trainer again. At the time, I didn't know that decision would be the catalyst to change the trajectory of my business and my life.

Within a month of returning to the gym, the nutritionist on staff was fired (big fight with the owner over the direction of the department is what I heard). I was asked to step into her role. Thank you, Universe. I thought... this is my big chance. I'm finally going to make it since I'm walking into a position with a full client load.

The joke was on me, again. The nutritionist who was there before me was running a knock-off version of the Zone Diet, which didn't include any of the assessments or protocols I was taught. Everyone got the same generic framework. She didn't really customize anything. Her way of doing things was so foreign to me that I couldn't wrap my mind around how to do it.

So I changed everything she had put together and put clients through the process I was taught in school. That turned out to be a huge mistake. It took *one whole day* before her clients started to ask for refunds because the plans I gave them were too hard to follow.

I was taught to offer a single session where I would assess the client using specific forms, and then I was supposed to go away and summarize their results and put together a plan for them. Doing that meant I had to spend hours of my own time devising meal plans, recipes, shopping lists, supplement recommendations, and instructions for the client to follow. All in all, creating one client plan took about five hours.

Then the client would come back for an hour-long follow-up, which was included in the initial fee, where together we would review the plan. They would then leave and follow the plan—or so I assumed. But that never happened because the plan was too intricate. But I didn't know any other way to work with clients, so I was just doing what I was taught.

But there was an even bigger problem beyond not knowing how to work with clients. I didn't know how to get clients. I was under the impression that I was going to be handed clients because I was working in a busy gym. Nope. While I did have access to the gym members, I was responsible for getting clients. And from my last experience at the chiropractor's, I already knew that I had no idea how to get clients, so I panicked.

No one taught me how to market my business beyond having a website, creating blogs, having brochures, offering free talks, and asking for referrals. But when you can't even get clients, it's pretty hard to ask for referrals! I had no idea how to talk about what I did or how I could help people, other than to say that I was a nutritionist.

What I quickly realized was that while I did have the knowledge to help clients, there was a gaping hole between my nutrition and health knowledge and how I was supposed to use that knowledge in my formal practice so that I could grow my business. It was like I was book smart but street dumb.

It also felt like what I had learned in school was completely inapplicable in the real world. There I was with these letters after my name, R.H.N., but with no framework or guidance about how to make use of them. To say that my self-esteem took a big hit is an understatement. I felt like a fraud. I felt like I was playing a role that I had no business playing.

And yet I wanted to feel legit and professional. I wanted to be able to prove to myself and my-then husband that I didn't have a 'hobby business', but that I was working with clients, getting them results, and bringing home an impressive paycheck. I enrolled in school because I wanted to be able to help people and because I wanted to turn this into a career.

At the rate I was going, none of that was happening. None of it, that is, until I had another extremely uncomfortable conversation—this time with my manager at the gym—that changed everything.

Chapter 2

HOW ALMOST GETTING FIRED SAVED MY BUSINESS

"*Lori*, can I speak with you for a minute?" Tara, my manager, had poked her head into my office; the look on her face made my stomach turn. I immediately started to scan through a list of things I might have done wrong. Did I fill out the sales report incorrectly? Did a client complain about me? I wracked my brain for things she could want to talk to me about. I don't know about you, but when someone in an authority position asks to speak with me, I immediately get scared like I'm in some kind of trouble.

In the 15 seconds I had to think about what I could have done that would warrant a 'talking to', I drew a blank. I had been at the gym for a couple of months, and although things were rocky at first, I thought they were getting better. I had a couple of new clients, and the free seminars I was hosting were well-attended. I was never able to get clients from them, but at least it was value-added for the gym members.

Tara and I had become friends over the last couple of months, but I could tell she wasn't standing in my office in a 'friend' capacity. She was there as my boss. And just like a good boss would, she started with the positives...

- I was doing better in the role.
- I was getting more clients.
- The personal trainers were starting to refer their clients to me.
- The gym members really loved the free seminars.
- But I knew there was a "but" coming...

"But—you're not hitting your monthly sales goals. When you took on this role, I was very clear that the nutrition department had its own sales goals and that in order for me to justify giving you this office space and not using it for something else, you'd have to hit your goals each month. The owner of the gym expects each department to hit their sales quota, and if they don't, I have to explain why and how we're going to make up for it next month. You've never hit your monthly sales goal. We're running a business here. You need to hit your goals."

Don't cry, Lori. Don't cry. That was the mantra I was repeating over and over in my head as words were coming out of Tara's mouth. I was working so hard. I was spending hours creating free content for the gym's website, my office window, and for the trainers to give to their clients. In addition, I was also creating content with handouts on a new topic for my twice-monthly free seminars. I also spent hours talking with members and giving them free advice. All this was in the hopes of getting clients, so when Tara told me that I wasn't hitting my sales goals, I got angry.

"What would you like me to do? I'm doing everything I know how to do. I create all this content, and nobody cares. Yeah, people attend my free talks, but nobody becomes a client afterwards. I sell an assessment and follow-up for $150. How would you like me to hit that number every month?" Then came the waterworks. Great. I just yelled at my boss and now I'm crying. Good job, Lori. Always the professional.

What happened next was a conversation for which I have been grateful every single day since. It was the first of a few conversations that would go on to change the trajectory of my business and my life. Tara handed me a tissue and asked, "Do you want to hit your monthly sales goals?"

"Of course," I said. "Why wouldn't I? But I can't because there is no way that I'll be able to work with enough clients charging what I charge to hit that number. I'll have to add more hours to my schedule, which means working more nights and adding another shift on the weekend."

"Why do you have to charge that amount? Why can't you offer packages like we do in the personal training department? Why can't you offer group programs and multisession 1:1 packages—just like we do for personal training? Why can't you change the way you do things?"

"Because I can't, Tara. It's not how I was taught. Nobody runs their nutrition practice that way. I wouldn't know how to change things, even if I wanted to, so I guess I'm just screwed."

In his book *See You at the Top*, Zig Ziglar talks about how "many people make the same mistake...because they blindly, without question, follow the crowd in a circle to nowhere. They follow methods and procedures for no other reason than 'it's always been done that way.'" He goes on to tell a story that made so much sense to me after the fact:

> In this respect, they are as bad as 'this old boy down home.' His wife sent him to the store for a ham. After he bought it, she asked him why he didn't have the butcher cut off the end of the ham. 'This old boy' asked his wife why she wanted the end cut off. She replied that her mother had always done it that way and that was reason enough for her. Since the wife's mother was visiting, they asked her why she always cut off the end of the ham. Mother replied that this was the way her mother did it; Mother, daughter, and 'this old boy' then decided to call grandmother and solve this three-generation mystery. Grandmother promptly replied that she cut the end of the ham off because her roaster was too small to cook it in one piece.

That's what I was doing. I was using the 'this is how it's always been done' rationale as the reason why I couldn't do things differently—I was too dependent on precedence. And it was keeping me stuck. Thank goodness Tara challenged me… "Seriously, Lori," she said. "Why can't you change what you're doing and how you're pricing it? Is there a reason?"

"No, Tara, there isn't a good reason aside from I don't even know where to begin."

Nobody I knew was running their nutrition business that way. Everyone was following the same model as I was, so there was no one I could ask for help.

I failed tenth grade math. It was the last math course I ever took. Numbers made me feel dumb. But had to stop ignoring them unless I was prepared to get fired, which I wasn't. So I sat down with Tara and a calculator and we did some math. We took the monthly sales goal and divided it by my current session rate of $150.

$5,000 / $150 = 33.3$

Instant tears. There was no way I had the time to see 33 new clients every single month. How was I even supposed to get that many? At that point, I was averaging two to three new clients a week, which meant I was working like a dog at home trying to get their programs created.

"Okay," I said. "Clearly this isn't going to work, so how do I change it?" And that was the question where it all began. I didn't know it at the time, but I had taken a huge leap, broken a false belief and made a mindset shift that would end up transforming my future.

"What if you offer a six-session package like we do in personal training? Six sessions at $75 each. That's $450 for each client, which means you'd only need 11 clients per month."

Okay, that sounded more reasonable. I could do that. 11 new clients every single month. So basically, I'd always be working with 22 clients at a time. "Um, T, that would mean that I need to work Monday to Thursday nights from 5:00 p.m. to 9:00 p.m., two morning shifts, and maybe even a weekend shift. I'll never eat dinner with my husband during the week."

She threw her hands up in the air and said, "Lori, figure it out. If you want to keep your job, figure it the fuck out" and walked out of my office.

Before we go any further, you should know something about me: I am a person who deeply believes that everything happens to me for a reason—even if I don't know what it is at the time, and even if the experience is dark and stormy. I don't think anything happens by chance, and over the years I've cultivated the belief system that as long as I just take the next step forward, I will be guided toward whatever it is I'm supposed to learn and whatever it is I'm supposed to do.

What if I scrapped the way I was taught to run my business and started from scratch? What if I made up the rules about what I could and could not do, based on what best suited me? Could I really do that? I mean… there were no 'nutrition police' around to stop me. So I started to brainstorm.

> What did I like about my job?
> What did I never want to do?
> How did I want to work with clients?
> How many clients could I handle at a time?
> What would be in the client's best interest?
> If I could control my schedule, what would that look like?
> How much time did I want to spend on administrative duties?
> Could I run my business in a way that got rid of individual client protocols?
> Who did I want to work with?
> How could I help them?
> How did I want to work with them?
> What could I learn about why clients want to work with me?

How was working with me different from working with a personal trainer?

How would I get clients?

How much money did I want to make?

And then I stopped. How much money did I want to make? *Hmm*, I'd actually never thought about it before. I had never sat down and created a budget or a plan for my business; I guess that's because I didn't know that I was supposed to. All I knew was the total amount of our mortgage and bills each month, so I tried to aim for that.

I never hit it, though.

I wrote down a number: $100,000. It felt huge and impossible to me. It's worth noting that the only reason I wrote down that number was because my best friend's husband is a lawyer and that's how much he was getting paid at the time. I had never had a corporate job, so I had no idea how much money people made. It's also worth noting that at the time I didn't know there was a difference between my business making $100,000 and me making that amount of money. I sat there and stared at that number. Could I really make $100,000? It felt like a big goal to strive for.

The next week was spent holed up in my office, researching and brainstorming, and totally avoiding Tara for fear of getting fired. That line, "we're running a business here" kept replaying in my mind. Wait, am I running a business? Is my nutrition practice a business? Am I a business owner?

Now don't laugh… I actually had those thoughts. Of course, I knew my nutrition practice was a business, but until that moment it didn't really sink in that I was responsible for the business as the business owner. In my head I was a registered holistic nutritionist, not a business owner. Except in reality I was both. And at the time, I was good at neither.

Then my alarm went off, and I realized it was time to go to my own small group session with my trainer. There were eight ladies in my group, and we were all at different fitness levels. The trainer had all of us doing the exact same movement, but she was able to modify it based on our own abilities. And then it clicked. As Oprah says, I had an 'aha!' moment.

I could do that. I could run nutrition classes exactly like this. I could put a bunch of women into a group session where they all had similar issues and give them all the same plan and just modify it based on their own unique circumstances. OMG. I figured it out. It was like the answer was downloaded directly into my brain. I ran out of the room and back to my office so I could write all my thoughts and ideas down before they disappeared. A brainstorm was flashing fast and furious. I was giddy because I knew in my bones that this idea would work.

And just like that it dawned on me... Weight Watchers. I could copy the Weight Watchers business. I mean, not the whole points system, but something similar. They ran groups. They put all kinds of women together and taught the program to all of them at once. This was in the Weight Watchers heyday where their physical locations were everywhere. So I joined Weight Watchers. I took notes on everything they did—what they said, what kind of materials I got, the questions they asked me, how they sold me into the program, the price of the program, how they ran their weekly groups, who led the groups, and how they taught the information. I felt like a spy who could get found out at any moment.

I spent two months attending Weight Watchers meetings, and by the time I was done, thanks to Weight Watchers and the table of contents of almost every fat-loss book out there, I had the first version of what would later become WOW! Weight Loss. And that program saved my job.

It was not long before I was sitting in my office with 12 chairs sprawled out in a semicircle. I was able to sell 12 spots into my program! I was shocked that 12 people signed up in the first place—and more so that they'd done it at $250 per person. I almost crapped my pants when I realized I had just made $3,000 for my department. Of course, Tara was thrilled because I was more than halfway to hitting my sales goal that month. And the best part about the whole thing was that I was working with 12 women for one hour per week. Not 12 women in 12 hours per week. 12 women for one, freaking, hour per week. And since the program I was walking them through was already created, I didn't have to spend five hours per client at home creating individual protocols. As I stood in my office and looked at those chairs I finally, after a year and a half of struggle, felt like I had arrived. Sure, I was nervous AF that the women wouldn't like me or get results, but the fact that I had just made $3,000 in, like, two days made me feel legit. No more 'hobby business' for me, thank you very much.

I gave that first iteration of the program everything I had. I supported those women like it was my job. I asked for so much feedback that I think they started to get annoyed with me. But I didn't care. This new way of running my nutrition practice was my meal ticket and I knew it. This new way of working with clients was going to be the way I made $100,000 without having to work every single night of the week and on weekends.

It turns out almost getting fired was the best thing that could have ever happened to me. It opened the door to opportunity.

Chapter 3

THE MODEL THAT GAVE ME A MULTIMILLION-DOLLAR **BUSINESS**

"*Hi*, Lori, see you tonight."

"Who's that?"

"Oh, that's Lori. She runs the WOW! program."

I had to walk past the cardio machines on the way to my office. I closed the door and did a happy dance. You know what I'm talking about—the one where you jump up and down and fist-pump the air because finally, finally, things feel like they're moving in a good direction.

We were in week six of the program. That week I had planned on talking about setting goals. I thought that was a good idea because we were halfway through the program, and I felt like the ladies needed a little injection of hope and motivation. We had talked about goals at the beginning of the program, so I wanted to circle back and check in. At that point in my career, I hadn't yet acquired any real coaching skills. I hadn't even thought of coaching as a concept. I had clients and I worked with clients. I taught them and gave them recommendations to follow. I assumed they would just follow them because they wanted to reach their goals. How naïve was I? You don't need to tell me now...

I started that week's session sharing very openly how the last year and a half had been a huge struggle for me personally. I was super honest about the failure at the chiropractic clinic and how I almost got fired and how this program that the 12 of them were in had literally saved me. I talked about why I went to nutrition school and why this job meant so much to me. I told them about my own goals, both personally and professionally. I definitely overshared with those women, but I felt so thankful to them. They took a chance on me. They paid $250 to work with me in a program that I made up sitting on the floor of Chapters bookstore (think Barnes & Noble), scanning through dozens of tables of contents. I wanted them to see that I had goals and dreams.

And I was hoping that if I shared mine, they would share theirs.

Up to that point, the weekly program consisted of a weigh-in, 20 minutes of teaching about a topic, a review of food journals, and the assignment of a new action task to focus on that week. I kept the tone light and friendly. But something changed that week. I can look back now and see exactly what I did to flip the switch because I've spent the years since then studying vulnerability, coaching, and client compliance. I went first. I was vulnerable first, and that transformed the group's energy.

Because I went first, I held space for my clients to follow. Because I went first, I created a tone where it was okay to share beyond the superficial. And one by one, each lady in my WOW! group started to talk about how she felt about her body and her weight. Some even shared their hopes for themselves and why they thought they gained the weight, which was incredible.

I had to quickly run out of the room to grab a tissue box because the tears were just flowing. I sat in my chair in complete awe (and also internally freaking out). I had no idea how to facilitate this. I had no idea how to support these women who were sharing some pretty deep stuff. I knew about candida, digestion, food labels, and macros. What did I say to a woman who was talking about how she hadn't been intimate with her husband in over a year because she was ashamed of her own body? I felt so out of my element. Where was the course in school that taught me how to be a therapist? All I could do in that moment was to give each person a hug and thank each person for sharing. Because of all the sharing that had just happened, we only had about seven minutes to focus on the goal-setting exercise—but it didn't matter. As the ladies were leaving, three of them came over to me and thanked me for the best session yet.

One said, "You have no idea how freeing it is to be able to talk about what's going on. I can't talk about this to anyone else because they just don't get it. Thank you for creating this program and for being open with your own feelings." Now this comment was coming from Judy, who up to this point I had been pretty sure hated me. She barely talked. She barely participated. And yet each week she showed up, got weighed, and submitted her food journal.

I misjudged her. All she needed was a safe space to open up. It was like she cracked the seal that evening.

After the ladies left, I sat on the floor in my office. Instinctually I needed to feel grounded. What had just happened? I was trying so hard to process it all, but it felt like my brain and my heart were running in opposite directions. One side of me felt like I was acting unprofessionally because I had overshared. I had been taught to be a professional—to assess and recommend, not to cry and share my passion, hopes, and dreams. But then the other side of me, the highly sensitive and intuitive side, was screaming at me: *This is what's really needed! Fuck the food labels, get them to honor their truth!*

But let me tell you, I was in no way equipped to handle all the feelings that were exposed in that session, even though I realized that talking about their experiences and their feelings was clearly a necessity if I wanted them to get the best possible results from my program. Once again, I was on my own to figure out how to truly support my clients over and above teaching them the fundamentals of proper nutrition. And since I had already broken the mold by creating a new way to run my practice, why not go all the way and completely shatter it? While teaching them about macros, fiber, stress, sleep, and how to handle social situations was important, that night's session made me see I was missing a whole side of the program that was more important.

I spent the entire next year growing my nutrition practice using one program—WOW! Weight Loss. I had a minimum of two groups, each with 12 women, going at any given time. One in the morning and one in the evening. I started to bump up against a problem, though. Some of the women didn't want to join the group or didn't want to wait until the next group started, so they would ask if they could do the program with me privately. *Hmm*, why not? What a good idea; thank you for thinking of it. So I also started to offer the WOW! Weight Loss program as a private 12-week program. Of course, I charged more for working 1:1 with me.

Before I continue telling you about how I filled the group programs and my 1:1 schedule, I should add here that at this point in my journey I also had a six-month-old daughter, Alexis. When you are self-employed, there is no option for maternity leave, and when your business is just picking up steam, you don't opt to take time off. The gym had a babysitting room and offered to keep my daughter during my work hours. Since I was able to plan my morning group time during her nap, I didn't feel as guilty.

But let me tell you, juggling both a growing business and a baby was no easy task. There were plenty of times when I ran into the gym and literally pushed that stroller into the babysitting room, wiped the sweat off my face, and entered my office to find all 12 ladies waiting for me. And of course, there were other times where Lita, the amazing woman who loved Alexis like she was her own, came to get me because she just couldn't settle her.

Honestly, I didn't realize it at the time—actually, I didn't realize it until I was typing these words—but even back in 2009, I had created my ideal scenario where I was attracting and working with my ideal clients, clients who never once complained about the interruptions. That meant I got to be a mom and grow a business at the same time. Fast forward a decade and nothing has changed. My kids are a big part of my brand and my company, and they most definitely still appear in my coaching sessions (sometimes I have to mute a session because the school is calling), and not once have I ever had a client complain about it.

So how did I do it? How did I create the WOW! Weight Loss program and fill all those groups and my 1:1 client schedule, given that I wasn't running my business the way I was taught in school? Back in 2009/2010, signature programs and funnels weren't a popular thing. Neither was having an online business. The platforms that we have today didn't exist, and I had no idea how to automate and leverage my time. I didn't even have an email marketing platform… I know, I know, how horrible, right? I was making the rules up as I went.

Remember, I was the one who didn't even realize I was growing a business, so I wasn't able to think methodically or strategically. Everything I did was either intuitive or in response to a problem. I was either jumping in head-first or putting out fires. And there were so many problems. The first was: how do I even get people to know I exist? Then there was the issue of actually getting clients on an ongoing basis. How do I get multiple clients to sign up at one time? How do I answer all their questions? How do I follow up with people who express interest but haven't paid? How do I get my new clients started? How do I check in with my clients throughout the program? What happens to those clients who have finished the program? What do they do after?

Books were the answer. Somewhere along the way, I figured out that there were books that I could buy at the bookstore that mostly taught me how to grow a business, how to market, and how to sell. So I went back to the bookstore and spent hundreds of dollars buying books on sales and marketing. I came home with bags of them. Buying those books was the first big investment I made in my business.

After a couple of weeks, I felt like Zig Ziglar, Verne Harnish, the author of Mastering The Rockefeller Habits, and I were in an intimate three-way relationship. I devoured those books. Except there was this one thing that kept frustrating me and made learning and actioning that knowledge so damn hard: none of those books were specifically applicable to what I was doing.

The books, as great and as helpful as they were, weren't about the alternative health industry, and they didn't spell out exactly how to solve my problems. So again, it was up to me to figure out how to put the framework they were teaching about general business into a usable format so I could grow my business and get clients.

But I did it. After much trial and error, I figured out how to reach the women I wanted to work with and have them pay attention to me. I fumbled my way through hosting talks. It didn't matter that the talks took place in the cardio studio. The menopausal ladies I wanted to work with would attend, and they'd bring their friends because what I was talking about was applicable. I taught myself how to create a talk that would position the program so I could sell *en masse* and how to ask for the sale in a confident way. I paid very close attention to what worked when it came to enroll them and how to follow up when I couldn't enroll them. I took every piece of feedback and criticism and used it to improve my program and get my clients better results. Those books gave me the business education that helped lay the foundation for what is now the Health Expert Business Model and a multimillion-dollar company.

I wrote this book for you because this is the book that I wish I had found in the bookstore all those years ago. I was so desperate for someone to acknowledge how hard it was to build my business and just to tell me what to do so that I could immediately put it into practice, but I didn't have that. I didn't have anyone to talk to or bounce ideas off of. I didn't have anyone to tell me the truth about what it was really like and how it wasn't just about working with clients in order to get to where I wanted to go. Nor did I have any time to question whether what I was doing was the right thing or not. I was literally making it up as I went along and hoping I wouldn't crash and burn.

But what I was doing was working. I was filling my groups and hitting my monthly sales goals.

And then something big happened. The owner of the gym asked me to offer my program in their second and third gym locations. By that point, I had things so systematized that it was easy to hire another nutritionist, train her, and have her facilitate my program. I taught her everything I knew and gave her the WOW! Playbook so she could just replicate my process step by step. Within two months she had two groups filled and was booking up quickly. I was onto something. It was unintentional at first; it was by necessity, but it was working. And it continues working to this day.

Since then, I have taken what I did to grow my nutrition practice and turned it into the Health Expert Business Model, which is the 5 +1 pillars I'm going to give you in this book. This is the model you will use to grow your business, get clients, and ditch your day job (or at least contribute to your household). I want this book to be your go-to guide, your personal cheerleader, and your back-pocket belief system. From this moment on, you and I are in this together, and I have your back. You are no longer alone on this journey.

Before we dive into the nitty-gritty, it's important that you have a clear understanding of your business. What I'm not going to do is give you a whole bunch of timely tactics or tips that work for five minutes until the algorithm changes and *bam*, you're out of luck and your business no longer works. I am going to teach you the core pillars comprising your business model so that you know how and when to use the mechanics, tactics, and strategies that will help your business to grow. It's supremely important to me that you become a knowledgeable and confident business owner. Even if you aren't right now. I want you to be able to tell the difference between smoke, mirrors, and vanity metrics (hello, number of Instagram followers) and a legit business operating from sound decisions that are made based on the goals, tracked numbers, and objectives of the business.

What I'm about to go through with you is the education I wish more than anything that I had received. It's not the hot, sexy, flashy stuff that excites most people. If you sit in a room with anyone making over $1 million, we're not talking about how many Instagram followers we have or how many comments a post got or whether our logo looks good or what to name a Facebook group. When I get in a room with these people, who are all doing multi-seven-digit figures per year or more (think eight), we talk about one or more of the 5 +1 pillars in some way, shape, or form. So do yourself a favor and stick with me here. Understanding and being able to action the 5 +1 pillars that make up the Health Expert Business Model will make or break your success.

The Health Expert Business Model

Don't disqualify yourself from this section just because you don't *think* it will work for your business, niche, designation, geographic location, or philosophy. Do your very best to keep an open mind and ask yourself, "How can I apply this to the mission and vision I created?" Come with a growth-oriented mindset. In my business I have worked with every single type of professional designation, business, and niche you can think of including medical doctors, registered dietitians, naturopathic doctors, functional medicine practitioners, registered nurses, licensed therapists, health coaches, energy healers, life coaches, sexologists, psychologists, cancer coaches, physiotherapists, marriage counselors, aromatherapists, direct sales people (essential oils/product sales), chiropractors, midwives, doulas… And the list goes on.

The Health Expert Business Model is made up of the 5 +1 pillars that all health and wellness businesses need in order to grow and scale. Think of your business like an ecosystem. A thriving ecosystem has a lot of different parts that work together to ensure its survival. A business functions in the same way. Without any one of the 5 +1 pillars, the business ecosystem will not thrive. Sure, it will exist, but it will have to work so much harder to grow than if all the parts were working symbiotically. Sometimes a certain part will flourish, sometimes a certain part will need more support, sometimes the ecosystem will maintain equilibrium, and other times it will need intensive support to prevent it from dying. The Health Expert Business Model functions the same way. It needs constant love, attention, care, and management because without these things, the ecosystem will cease to exist.

The 5 +1 Pillars Explained:

I'm going to give you a high-level overview of the Health Expert Business Model. Then I'm going to spend the rest of this book breaking down each of the 5 +1 pillars for you. If what I explain in this section isn't super clear to you yet, just stick with me. I promise that by the time you're done with this book, you won't even be able to recognize your business or yourself (but in a really good way).

The Health Expert Business Model gives you tangible actions so that you can attract the people you want to work with the most and guide them through the prospect-to-client journey. The 5 +1 pillars give you the framework so you can grab a complete stranger's attention and turn them into a client in a systematic and repeatable way. Pretty cool, right?

The Critical +1 Pillar: Who Do You Want to Serve? (Nail This or Risk Failing)

You should create your brand, business, and all of your programs with a singular purpose: to attract and work with a specific type of person who has a specific type of problem. This person is called an *'ideal client'*. Everything that you create in your business—your logo, fonts, colors, blog content, social media content, videos, Facebook group name, your program, and the outcome the program provides—are all reverse-engineered based on who you want to work with the most and the problem you solve for them.

My ideal client was a menopausal woman who wanted to lose weight but couldn't and didn't want to give up wine, chocolate, and popcorn. I chose 'menopausal women' because at that point in my life, my mother was dealing with these struggles and since I was able to help her, I knew I could help other women like her. I knew everything about her, and because of that, I was able to connect with her via my brand and content in a way that caught her attention and motivated her to want to know more about how I could help her.

If you don't clearly define who your brand and business are for, everything you create will be confusing, muddled, unclear, and honestly, a waste of time. Defining your ideal client before you do anything (and I mean *anything*) is critical because everything you create comes from knowing your ideal client and the problem that they have and want so badly to solve. Without this focus, you'll always feel like you're grasping at straws and on the hamster wheel running around in circles in search of your next client. And, of course, the hamster never gets anywhere.

After you define your ideal client, you'll be able to create and implement the remaining five pillars that make up the Health Expert Business Model.

Pillar 1: How to Stand Out from the Crowd

Now that you know who you want to work with the most and the problem they have, you will create content that resonates with them (versus writing fluff pieces that get passed over, like "five ways to stay hydrated" or "how to make overnight oats"). You'll use content like blogs, social media, video, etc. to talk to your ideal client to get their attention and draw them into your world so that you can guide them down the pipeline into the next pillar.

Pillar 2: The KLT + E Sequence

This is the most-often overlooked pillar, but it's important because it sets the prospect up for the next phase. KLT + E stands for Know, Like, Trust, and Engage. At this point your ideal client is in your world (they're on your email list and consuming your content), but they don't really know you yet. Stranger danger is still at max level. So it's your job to build rapport and get them to know, trust, and like you by creating edu-taining content that nurtures them and gets them ready to move to the next pillar. If they don't know, trust, and like you, it won't matter how good your program is—you won't get the 'YES!' you're looking for.

Pillar 3: Getting the YES!

This is the part where most practitioners and coaches lose it. I'm not going to sugarcoat it. This is the sales conversation. This is where you engage in a two-way conversation to determine if the person is a good fit to work with. This isn't a conversation where you hope and pray that they say 'yes' because you need the money. It's important to note that if you've done pillars +1, 1, and 2 correctly, this conversation shouldn't feel salesy at all. It should feel supportive and should result in a 'yes' from both of you most of the time.

Pillar 4: Build the Methodology (The Signature Program)

Now you have a new client. Yay! How are you going to provide the outcome you promised them in a reliable, repeatable, and scalable way? It's easy: you're going to create an automated signature program that you will put all your ideal clients through. Now before you get all, "But Lori, it won't work because of X" on me, remember that you promised to come with a growth mindset. I'll allay all your objections in Chapter 9, the one dedicated to this pillar. All you need to understand right now is that the way to growing your business, getting clients, and ditching your day job is to have an automated signature program that solves a problem your ideal client has.

Pillar 5: Keep Clients for Life

"What about working 1:1 with clients, Lori? What happens to my clients after they go through my signature program? How do I personalize the signature program for them?" All these are good questions addressed by this pillar. Before clients can do the deep work that comes with personalized 1:1 care, it's important that they nail down the fundamentals. Most will still be failing at that. Think of it this way: the signature program is based on working through the fundamentals. Only once they excel at those can you enroll the client into a more personalized program that allows you to dive deeper and allows them to continue to receive your support as they go through their healing journey.

How to Use This Book

It's important that you work through this book sequentially, as each pillar builds on its predecessor. If you skip steps, you skip success. You be tempted to jump ahead because you think one pillar is inapplicable to you. Maybe it's too challenging or it's boring for you. But trust me, don't. Neither of us want your business to come crumbling down like a house of cards.

While reading this book, it's important to pay attention to your self-talk, and your feelings. Is the reason you're not following the steps because you don't understand them or because fear is rearing its ugly head?

I have a mantra in my community that I'm pretty sure I got from listening to hundreds of hours of Abraham Hicks: "Always take the path of least resistance." Pair that with, "Always take imperfect action", and you'll be set. We're not striving for perfection, so let's just take that off the table. Work through the whole book once. I've included prompts and examples to help you so that you're rarely starting with a blank page. By the time you're done with this book, you will have the tangible components that make up your business so that all you'll need to do is fill in the gaps. Basically, this book is the roadmap to growing your online business so that you can work with the people you most want to work with, transform their lives, and in return transform yours.

It doesn't matter where you're starting from or how much client experience you have or don't have. The Health Expert Business Model is the framework you will use to build, grow, and get clients. You'll come back to it again and again as you work to transform yourself into the expert and business owner you deserve to be.

Blocks That Might Stop You from Taking Action:

This isn't the first time I've taught the Health Expert Business Model. I've been teaching it for years, and so I am extremely well-versed in the blocks and challenges that will rear their head as you try and put yours down to work.

I'm going to address these blocks here so that hopefully we can get ahead of them and so that when/if one or more of these thoughts or feelings come up for you, you are well prepared to handle them in the healthiest and most productive way possible so that you can continue to take massive imperfect action.

Block # 1: I Need Client Experience Before I Start Building My Business.

No, you don't. It's completely understandable that you don't feel confident, but that's simply because you don't have client experience. So instead of investing in more courses, hoping that you'll find confidence there, just start working with clients. Own the fact that you are just starting out and that you are new to working with clients. That doesn't mean that you don't know what you're doing. It just means that you're new to working with clients. Let's not attach any more meaning to you just getting started than there needs to be.

Later in the book, I'm going to explain the concept of collecting feedback on your signature program, which gives you the opportunity to work with clients in a "test" capacity. Hopefully knowing that allows you to breathe a sigh of relief.

Block # 2: I Don't Know What I'm Doing or If It Will Work.

That's why you're reading this, my friend. Of course you don't have any proof of concept that your idea or vision will work.

No one does when they're starting out! It's okay to be skeptical. However, all you need to do is look on the internet to see that there are many other people already doing what you want to do. There is proof all around you that 'it' will work. The real problem, frankly, isn't so much that you aren't sure if 'it' will work. It's that you don't wholeheartedly believe that you can do it. Am I right? I think I am, only because I once held that false belief too. It's complete and utter nonsense. The fact that you're reading this book right now and have committed to going through it and doing the work tells me that you have what it takes, even if you feel scared. Throughout this book I'm also going to show you case studies of practitioners who, just like you, started their businesses with no clue about what they were doing and who are now making five or six figures a year.

Block # 3: Why Would Someone Pay Me When There Is So Much Free Information Available?

Yes, there is so much free health, fitness, and lifestyle information on the internet, and that does serve its purpose. But it's not going to help your clients get the results they desire. The reason someone is going to pay to work with you is because you have a specific methodology that will solve their specific problem. People pay for that specificity because they identify with it so much more strongly than a generic web-post or cure-all diet regime—it provides them with a level of certainty. And by the time you're done with this book, you'll have that top-tier product. Then it's about making sure that you communicate that to your audience. The fact that the market is full of other people doing something similar is actually a good thing. It means there's a demand, which is awesome for you. The other reason why people will pay you (and this might be the most important one) is because they actually want to work with you. Because of the way I'm going to teach you to set up and grow your business, your audience will quickly get to know, trust, and like you, and they're going to want to pay to work with you.

Block # 4: I Don't Have Time, or Now Isn't the Right Time.

If there is one thing I know for sure, it's that there will never be a right time to focus on growing your business. Life will never pause, and anything can happen at any time. Not having time to work on your business is a choice. I'm sure if you evaluated what you did for 15-minute intervals throughout the day, you'd be able to secure at least 30 minutes to an hour per day to work on your business. There's this big misconception that you need to be working 16 hours a day on your business in order to grow it. That is simply not true. Whatever time you have is enough. It has to be. What other choice do you have? So instead of using the "I don't have enough time" or "now isn't the right time" excuse, why not use that energy to figure out how to carve out time each week and secure it so that you aren't in the same spot a year from now, hoping that there will be more time then?

Block # 5: I'm Not Good at X
(Tech, Sales, Writing, Marketing, Numbers).

My son plays hockey every single chance he gets. He wakes up in the morning and goes outside (in the garage in the winter). He's on the ice at least six to eight hours a week. He has extra training practices monthly. If I let him skip school to play hockey, he would. Sometimes when I go outside to check on him, I find a water bottle on the top right or left side of the net. "What's that there for, Daniel?" I ask.

"I have to knock the water bottle down. It means I hit the target. Top shelf right or left corner. I'm practicing. Connor McDavid takes one hundred shots on each side every day."

Want to know what you do when you're not good at something? You practice, like Daniel does. Over and over again. You make it your mission to learn how to do it better. Of course you don't feel like you're good at sales or writing or whatever yet. How many hours have you put in?

During coaching calls with our clients, I often get requests for help to improve sales conversations. The first question I ask is, "how many calls have you done?" If the answer is fewer than 20, I don't offer any feedback. Go and do 20. Listen to the recordings. Critique yourself, and then let's talk. You haven't fired enough shots yet to know what you're doing wrong.

The truth is, and I think you already know this, that the first dozen or so times you do anything, it will suck. It's not good. The first version of the WOW! Weight Loss program I created was horrible. But guess what? I could have never made it better if I didn't have the first version. Give yourself a break, okay? You're just learning. As long as you don't quit, you will get better.

And while this isn't a block per se, it's worth talking about here: *fear*. I love this breakdown of the word "fear":

False
Emotion
Appearing
Real

Fear, or Resistance, as I like to refer to it, can stop you dead in your tracks. It can have such a hold on you that it feels hard to breathe. The emotion of Resistance is something I've struggled with my entire career, so I feel somewhat qualified to speak to it.

According to Steven Pressfield, author of the book *The War of Art* (read it), "Resistance is a universal force that acts against human creativity. Its sole mission is to sabotage aspirations."

Let's examine that last line again: Fear/Resistance's sole mission is to sabotage aspirations. It's critically important for you to become acutely aware of your own Resistance so that you can identify it when it shows up and tries to knock you off course. There are rituals, habits, and strategies you can use to acknowledge and process through the Resistance so that you can continue to take imperfect action.

Here are some ways Resistance might show up for you:

- Not sticking to your weekly plan and making

exceptions to help others that then delay your work deadlines
- Not being able to make a decision for fear of making the wrong one
- Finding all kinds of excuses about why you can't focus on your work
- Jumping from idea to idea without ever really getting started
- Starting too many projects but never seeing any of them all the way through to completion
- Asking for or listening to the opinions of your family and friends as if they were the truth
- Overbooking your calendar with things you don't really want to do so that you don't have time to do the work you know you need to do because it pushes you outside of your comfort zone
- Filling your day with busy work or menial tasks that don't really have anything to do with growing your business

The minute I open my eyes, I feel the Resistance. I mean, I don't really want to get out of bed at 5:00 a.m., but I do it anyway. My days are usually so meticulously planned out that I don't give myself time to think. I just do what's on my schedule. Sure, there are tasks that I procrastinate over because I don't like doing them, but I've conditioned myself into doing the things that need to get done first, whether I like them or not, because they must get done.

For me, Resistance looks like this:

- Having a gazillion ideas that I feel like I must implement now. I used to be (I'm so much better now) notorious for constantly switching directions, adding in new projects, and stopping others.
- Pushing back deadlines until the very last second.
- Feeling anxiety, especially in the form of nervousness specific to an issue or something I don't want to deal with that I know I must.
- Trying to come up with an alternative way to do something simply because I can't bring myself to do it.

We all experience a level of Resistance. The issue is whether we give it power or not. When I start to feel the Resistance creeping in, I immediately go back to the vision I created for my business and life. I constantly remind myself of my business's mission and my personal vision—of where I'm headed and why it's important to me.

In her book *Big Magic*, Elizabeth Gilbert wrote a letter where she acknowledges fear as part of the family. Fear is allowed to have a seat—but in the back seat—and under no circumstances is it ever allowed to drive. Fear and Resistance are part of the package, and they'll always be there. But the goal is to be able to acknowledge them for what they are and move forward with courage, determination, and resilience. Building a business isn't for the faint of heart, but the rewards, both personal and financial, are oh-so worth it.

Ready to get started? Let's go ...

Chapter 4

LAY A SOLID FOUNDATION TO GROW FROM

"*Of* course you can. It won't be easy, but of course you can," Bedros, my business coach, said. His response to me was so matter of fact that it almost took my breath away. I will never forget this conversation as it set the stage for what has become my business and my life.

I was sitting in the backyard of a beautiful Costa Mesa, California home, surrounded by other fitness and health professionals. We were masterminding (collectively sharing our businesses and getting mentored), and we were asked to create a big audacious mission that would become the focus of our businesses for the next 10 years.

I need to admit that I was a bit blown away by the idea of planning for 10 years. A decade... it felt like a very long time. What if I couldn't focus on one thing for that long? What would I do? But then I started to understand the importance and the implications of the exercise. It was to get us to create a mission for our business, something that went beyond the money. It was meant to be something we felt purpose-driven to achieve so that the mission itself would motivate us to continue to push forward when the going got tough.

It's funny how I thought 10 years was such a long time back then. I had that conversation in 2012.

So, my mission: help 1 million people transform their health. And the way I was going to do that was by directly working with 1,000 health professionals and helping them to each work with 1,000 clients. That would mean that I, although indirectly, would impact 1 million people by 2022. I called it my 1M Mission.

At that point in my business-building journey, I wasn't sure if it was possible for me to work with 1,000 clients. It felt like an overwhelming number of people. I had no idea how I was going to do that. But I made that my mission, so I knew that I had to figure it out. And figure it out I did. We achieved that mission years ago.

One of the most important, helpful, inspiring, and motivating actions I've ever taken was to create that mission for my business as well as a vision for what I wanted my business and life to look and feel like. It makes me a little sad that I didn't do this right after I graduated. But better late than never, right?

Before we dive into the 5 +1 pillars of the Health Expert Business Model, it's important to lay a solid foundation by creating a mission for your business and a vision for your business and life so that you have concise, strong motivators to keep you taking imperfect action, especially when the going gets tough (because it will, more than once).

It's been my experience that practitioners and coaches graduate from school and just dive into building their websites and setting up their social media pages—so on and so on without taking time to first lay a solid foundation from which to work. It's like hiring an architect to build you a house and only having paint colors and throw pillows picked out. In order for the architect to build you the house of your dreams, you need to have a clear vision for what you want it to look like, how you want it to function, the style, etc. You basically need to be able to visualize the entire house in your mind and then communicate it to the architect so they can go and build it. The paint and throw pillows are the last additions.

How do you know what business you're going to build if you haven't stopped to think about it? What are you working toward? What do you want your business to look and feel like three to five years from now? I get that your thoughts right now are probably consumed with getting clients and making money. I get that you likely feel a lot of pressure to start building your business. But not having a clear mission and vision for your business will lead to confusion and the inability to confidently communicate what you do and who you serve. It will lead to the exact scenario you're so afraid of—not being able to get clients—because if you're unclear about the intention of your business, how do you expect potential clients to be clear?

At the end of 2015, my marriage officially ended. We were separated prior to that and reconciled for a short time. But then in December of 2015 we were done. My kids were seven and four at the time. I had just closed the doors to my nutrition practice because my online business had grown so fast that it had replaced my nutrition income, but to me that nutrition practice represented stability. It didn't help that I had a live event with hundreds of attendees that was scheduled in six weeks, and my life had imploded. It didn't help that at the time my now ex-husband was a significant part of my brand.

The morning after the decision was made, I called my business coach. He was the first person I called. "Hi Bedros... my marriage is over. My live event is coming up in six weeks, and my husband is a big part of my brand. I don't want to discuss my breakup with anyone, and it would be weird if he wasn't there. How do I handle this without having a complete meltdown?"

His response was the exact reminder I needed: "You created the event to be of service. This event is about them. Not you. Your job is to show up for them. Do that in whatever way you need to right now. Deal with your shit after."

The show must go on... and it did. Maybe you were at that live event back in 2016. Maybe you saw how much makeup I had on. The only memory I have from that event is my daughter saying to me, "Mommy, you don't look like you. You have so much makeup on."

"I know, lovey, it's my protective mask. I need it to hide what's really going on so people can't see how much I'm hurting" is what I wanted to say to her. But I didn't. I just laughed it off.

To say the next several weeks were hard is the understatement of a lifetime. I chose not to fall apart. I dealt with whatever I needed to. I asked God for things to be easy and effortless. I decided that since I had to go through this turmoil again, it was going to be quick, easy, and as painless as possible. I assumed everything would work out as it needed to for my best benefit. Then I released control and let the chips fall.

The night before the Wellness Business Summit started, I signed the mortgage papers with a 30-day close on the house I now live in. While at the hotel reception desk, I faxed the legal agreement back to my real estate agent. How's *that* for manifesting!

I'm not kidding when I tell you that the mission and the vision I created saved me. Oh, that and lots of therapy. But thank goodness I created that mission and the vision for how I wanted my business and life to look and feel like in 10 years, because that is what I focused on. Every single day for months, I read that vision statement I wrote out by hand. I focused on that. I didn't focus on what I no longer had or how far I still had to go; I focused on what I was building. The mission and vision I possessed kept me on track. It kept me motivated. It kept me inspired. I knew where I was going, with or without a husband, and I knew in my bones why it mattered.

Look, I'm not going to BS you and tell you that all will be smooth sailing from this moment on as long as you have a mission and vision statement. In fact, I can guarantee it won't be. But when shit hits the fan, because it most certainly will at some point, I want you to remain steadfast and focused because the dream you have to impact other people's lives matters. The goals you set for yourself matter, and they shouldn't be tossed aside because life sucks.

So before we dive into the sexy stuff like defining who you want to work with, the type of program you're going to offer, how you're going to stand out from the crowd, and all that good stuff, we need to lay a solid foundation from which you can grow. We need to focus on your ideas and your energy. We need to establish an end goal for your business so that we can work backward and create a plan to achieve it.

Let's look at the three core concepts that gave me clarity, focus, and daily motivation. You'll use these core concepts to help you build out your version of the Health Expert Business Model. These might seem trivial. They are not. They are powerful and should not be taken lightly. Depending on where you are in your business-building journey, this might be the first time you conceptualize the mission and vision for your business and your life. That's okay. These are fluid concepts that you can edit and modify over time. All we're doing right now is laying the foundation so that you have a mission and vision to work toward.

Concept # 1: You Are NOT Your Business

I know this might sound weird, but you are not your business. Yes, you are the expert, the leader, and the founder. And yes, it's your vision that you will be turning into a reality, but you as a human being are not the business. The business exists as an entity outside of yourself. This is an important concept to grasp and to remind yourself of daily. Why? Because your self-worth should not fluctuate based on the kind of day the business has. The business, as is typical for businesses, will have good days and bad days. There will be times when it feels like the bad days outnumber the good days, and when those days happen, I want you to be able to separate yourself from the business.

Over the last 20 years of growing my business, I've learned that I'm responsible for how I feel, and those feelings shouldn't be dependent on how the business is doing. My self-worth isn't tied to the profit and loss statement; it's tied to my actions. So as long as I'm doing everything in my power to support the business, then it's a good day, even when it's a bad day for the business. The name of this game is energy management. You need to maintain your energy because you are running a marathon. You need to build up your endurance so you can withstand the miles.

With that being said, there will be days when you aren't happy with your actions—maybe because you're tired or you're just having a bad day. That's okay. You're allowed to have a bad day; you're human. The good news is that you're in control, and if you are unhappy with something, you can work to fix it. Sometimes that's not the case with the business. Sometimes, with the business, things happen that are beyond your control. And when that happens, it's important for you to be able to reflect on your actions and know that you are doing everything you can to move the business forward.

The tools I'm going to give you in this book will help you to build up your endurance and resilience and teach you to focus on performing the actions that will grow your business and get you clients. If you focus solely on the outcomes without taking into consideration your efforts, you'll most likely always feel defeated—and I assume you don't want to feel like that.

So remember that you are not your business. You are a human being deserving of success.

Concept # 2: Create a Mission for Your Business

Before we can create a mission for your business, it's important to understand the definition and purpose of a mission. A mission defines what the business is currently doing and sets out its objectives.

A mission should be feasible and attainable. It should be clear and concise so that anyone reading can understand it. Whether they choose to join it or not, they know exactly what it is. And yet above all else, a mission should be inspiring, so that you feel excited and purpose-driven to achieve it.

A mission isn't, "I am a nutritionist and I can help you make better food choices."

I want you to think about the mission of your business. Ask yourself these two questions as a starting point. There are no right or wrong answers. The goal of this exercise is to get you to think about your business in a focused way so that you have an endpoint to work toward.

Who do you want to help?

What do you want to achieve?

When I talk with practitioners and coaches, they tell me that they want to work with people who have irritable bowel syndrome (IBS) or acne. Or with people who want to lose weight or reduce autoimmune pain or improve their child's behavior. My next question is always, "What do you want to help them with? What is the desired outcome?"

Exercise
for Creating a Mission for Your Business

Here's a template you can use to create your mission statement for your business. Remember, you can always modify it.

The mission of [name of business] is to help/support [specific person with a specific problem] to overcome/beat/get rid of [symptoms they experience] so that they can [describe the outcome that they want].

Now I want you to take 20-30 minutes, not longer, and come up with a mission statement for your business. Don't overthink it. It's not going to be perfect. You will most likely come back and improve it. But if you don't focus your ideas at the outset, it will be extremely difficult for you to work through the Health Expert Business Model because your business isn't for everyone.

Concept # 3: Create a Vision for Your Business (and Life)

Now that you have a mission statement created for your business, it's time to create a vision statement. Essentially, the vision statement sets out the impact you want to have in your corner of the world. It describes what you want to accomplish. It's a descriptive word picture of what success and impact look and feel like to you. I've put my own twist on creating a vision statement to add the "feeling" part. It's important for you (and me) to have goals. Of course, I'm all about the hustle, but if you aren't careful, you'll hustle and grind yourself into the ground. It is possible to achieve the level of impact and success you desire and to feel good most of the time during the process.

Often the vision is harder to create than the mission because creating a vision requires you to think big. I know that when I was starting my nutrition practice, thinking past how I was going to pay next month's bills was a big challenge, so it's understandable if this exercise feels like it's stretching you. It's good to stretch, but don't stretch too far outside of your comfort zone because you need to believe that the vision you want to create for your business and life is possible for you to achieve.

I want to give credit where credit is due. Years ago, I read Danielle LaPorte's book, *The Desire Map*. In it she describes creating "goals with soul." She explains that the essence of the goal, of what you desire to happen, *is* the feeling. How many people do you know who have achieved a certain level of success and impact but are miserable? I know loads. And I don't want that for you; it is possible to reach for more in a way that feels better as and when you achieve it, but in order to do that you must first get very intentional about your goals and how you want to feel as you work to turn your vision into a reality.

Over the years I've used both the company's mission and vision as guideposts. When ideas come, or when opportunities are presented to me, or when I feel out of alignment, I refer to the mission and vision. Is the idea, opportunity, or thing I'm working on bringing me closer to actualizing my mission or vision, or is it pulling me further away? If the answer is the latter, I redirect myself. Having a mission and vision are core concepts that will help guide you and keep you on track.

Exercise for Creating a Vision for Your Business (and Life)

Pick a date in the future—I suggest three to five years from now—and write the answers to the following questions in the first person as if they have already happened. This means you're writing in the present tense.

The date is: _____

The location is: _____

Big accomplishment # 1: _____
I am grateful to: _____
I am grateful for: _____
I feel: _____

Big accomplishment # 2: _____
I am grateful to: _____
I am grateful for: _____
I feel: _____

Big accomplishment # 3: _____
I am grateful to: _____
I am grateful for: _____
I feel: _____

I am proud of myself because: _____
_____
_____

The big accomplishments could be business or personal. I suggest doing two business-related and one personal.

Here's an example of my vision statement:

The date is July 2022, and I am sitting on the back deck of my four-bedroom cottage overlooking Lake Simcoe, sipping coffee with my husband. My children and stepchildren are inside playing a boardgame. I feel calm, secure, and at peace.

My family and friends are coming up soon so that we can celebrate the business hitting a major milestone. We reached our mission of turning one hundred practitioners into six- and seven-figure business owners. I am so grateful to my team who believed in what we were doing and who showed up to work every day ready to support, coach, and love our clients. I am grateful for the community of clients who worked hard to achieve their own goals. I feel proud and excited to be working with such an amazing group of leaders.

We're also celebrating the Lily Foundation reaching its milestone of having one million dollars in funding available to disburse to charities around the world. I am so grateful to the corporate donors that we've partnered with over the years to make this goal happen. I am grateful for our Lily team who never once stopped believing in our mission. I feel empowered that we're able to support so many women fulfilling their dreams of getting a quality education.

And lastly, we're celebrating our anniversary. I am so grateful to my husband who accepts me just as I am and who every single day works to become a better man for himself and for our family. I am grateful to God for bringing him into my life. I feel loved unconditionally and so incredibly grateful that I get to do life with this man.

I am proud of myself because throughout all of the dark moments I never stopped believing in myself and the business and life I could create, all on my own terms.

When I first wrote this vision statement, I have to admit I only sorta believed that it would come true, but I wrote it anyway. What you're reading in this book is an updated version, but the bones of it are still the same. As you can tell, I wrote a very specific vision that includes specific goals I want to hit and how I want to feel—calm, grounded, secure, impactful, and empowered.

The vision statement for my business and life you just read includes my company's current mission statement, which we're still working toward at the time of writing this book. I'll update my vision statement when we hit it. I hope that you can see how powerful it can be having mission and vision statements. They give you clarity and focus and goals to keep you on track as you work to grow your business.

Before you move on to the next pillar, I highly recommend that you take time to create your own mission and vision statements using the prompts in this section. You'll use them over and over again as you work through the Health Expert Business Model.

Chapter 5

Pillar #1:
WHO DO YOU WANT TO SERVE? (NAIL THIS OR RISK FAILING)

Wanna know a secret? The way you were taught to grow your business is dead wrong. I know it's a bold thing to say but it's true. I have 20 years and thousands of clients' worth of experience to back up this claim. Learning how to work with a client as a practitioner is not the same thing as learning how to grow a business. And it's not the school's fault. They are not responsible for your business success. They are responsible for your practitioner success—and in that sense, they've done their job.

Contrary to what you've been told, getting clients isn't about having a website, lots of social media followers, or a big email list. I know plenty of people who have all that and they're broke. Nor is it all about the software you use, the funnels you have, the webinars you host, or the Facebook ads you run.

The reality is that there is no shortage of practitioners and coaches trying to grow an online business. The market is competitive and that isn't going to change any time soon, so you need a solid strategy to stand out from the crowd so you can get clients. Without that solid strategy, you'll end up wasting loads of time and feeling like a failure. The good news is that the chances of that being your fate are slim because we are now besties and you've got this book in your back pocket.

The key to growing your business, standing out from the crowd, and getting clients is to set up your business *to serve one type of person* (of which there are hundreds of thousands) who has a specific problem that your program can fix. Remember back to when you were creating your mission for your business? I asked you a couple of questions, and one of them was, "Who do you want to help?"

Everything—and I mean literally everything—you're about to create from this point forward should be focused on talking to, educating, attracting, and working with one specific type of person, the person you want to work with the most. We're going to call this person your ideal client. The mission of your business is to serve and transform the lives of your ideal clients and nobody else.

Stick with me here because I know niching your business to only serve a specific type of person might feel contradictory to what you've been taught. I know that when I was in school, I learned a little bit about a lot of different elements of nutrition, health, and lifestyle. I wasn't taught to specialize or niche in any one single area, and I now believe that not doing so was one of the biggest mistakes I made when I was starting out. By trying to be a good nutritionist for everyone at once, I inadvertently made it really hard to work with anyone. But I remember the day that all changed.

"Hi, I see that you're a holistic nutritionist. I'm wondering if you can help me. I have Crohn's." I distinctly remember getting this voicemail because I felt torn. On the one hand, I could have figured out how to help this potential client, but I knew better by this point. I was not the best person to help her, even though I probably could have. So I called her back to let her know that I didn't have expertise in this area and that I wouldn't be the best person to help her; then I referred her to a colleague who would be much better suited to support her.

Just because I could have helped her doesn't mean that I should have, especially since I had never worked with anyone with Crohn's and didn't have the first clue how to go about supporting her. Sure, I learned a little bit about how to handle bowel disease in my professional training, but at that point I knew that even if I spent a dozen hours researching and putting together a program for her, it wasn't in her best interest to work with me because I was not an expert in Crohn's. I chose to stay in my macros, calories, and weight loss lane.

When someone has a problem they no longer want to have, what do they do? They type the specific problem into a Google search. They're looking for a professional who can help them get rid of their specific problem. Imagine for a minute that someone who is experiencing IBS types into Google "how to get rid of IBS" and they come across you and another practitioner who specifically deals with IBS. Whose social media page or website do you think they're going to click on?

The one who advertises a solution to the problem they have, right?

I understand that it might feel scary to narrow down your business to focus on just one specific type of person with a specific type of problem—you think that you'll miss out on working with clients. But the opposite is true. You will miss out on working with clients because you aren't specific enough in who your business is for and how you can help them because there will always be someone else who offers specific help for that specific problem, and that person will be the one who gets chosen over you.

Marie Forleo says, "If you're talking to everybody, you're talking to nobody." I want to make sure that your business is set up to stand out and attract only the people who you most want to work with. Go back to your mission: who do you want to help? The mission for your business is focused on helping one specific type of person—and remember, there are hundreds of thousands of them out there—so let's do away with the old line of thinking that you'll miss out on opportunities by narrowing down your focus. Because it is patently false.

Before you start to think about your brand, your social media, your website, or the program you want to create, you need to define your ideal client because nothing else in your business will work until you nail this. That's why it's the +1 pillar in the Health Expert Business Model.

You MUST know your ideal client better than you know your best friend.

Defining your ideal client and creating an in-depth, well-rounded ideal client profile *must* be the starting point when it comes to growing your business, getting clients, and making money. Think of it this way: if you don't know who your business is for, who you can help, and how you're going to help them, then what content are you going to create? How are you actually going to work with clients and get them results? How are you going to build a community? How are you going to make money? If you've ever sat down to create a blog post or a social media post and didn't know what to write about or if you've ever tried to create a program but weren't sure what content to include, that's because you didn't have a clear ideal client profile. If you did, you wouldn't have those problems. You aren't here to help all the people, just the ones you want to work with the most.

Ideal Client Profile: A detailed demographic and psychographic description of the specific type of person you most want to work with.

A big mistake most practitioners and coaches make is that they think they know their ideal client because they know the niche they work in and the symptoms their ideal client has. So they work really hard creating content and a program and promoting... And all they hear back are the crickets. Nothing. No new clients.

It's not enough to know your niche and your client's symptoms. You need to read your ideal client's mind. You must become obsessed with understanding them beyond their age, gender, marital status, and symptoms. You should want to know all about their life, their personality, their sense of humor, their fears, their deepest secrets, their hopes, their ideals, their mistakes, their self-defeating beliefs, and their desired outcomes. Robert Collier said, and this is critical:

> *"Always enter the conversation already taking place in the customer's mind."*

What is the first thing they think about when they wake up in the morning? What do they think about when they look in the mirror? What are their thoughts as they're getting dressed, putting on makeup, working, and spending time with loved ones? What do they wish they could do or experience? What thoughts keep them up at night? What is stopping them from living the fulfilled, healthy, and happy life they desire to have?

You need to move beyond the symptoms so that you will know how your ideal client thinks, feels, and acts so that you can create content that resonates with them. This is how you stand out in the crowded marketplace. At the end of the day, all your ideal client wants—all anyone wants—is to feel understood. When you create content that speaks directly to your ideal client's current experience, they will choose you because they will see that you get it. And that instills hope that you can help them.

So how do you go about creating an ideal client profile?

Your ideal clients all share similar characteristics, but it's helpful when creating your profile to think of just one person. As you work through this section, you'll start to conceptualize a person. Name them. Visualize what they look like and how they act. This way when you go to create content to get their attention, you can focus on writing just to them. It might seem weird, but trust me, it works.

Identify the Demographics

Age:
Gender:
Geographic location:
Education:
Hobbies:
Stores they shop at:
Brands they like:
Associations or organizations they belong to:
Symptoms they complain about the most:

It's important to note here that their age and gender (or any of the other demographics) might not matter when it comes to defining your ideal client. You might be able to define your ideal client based on only their symptoms and psychographics (I'll explain what these are below). I've added your ideal client's symptoms to the demographics part because, as I mentioned before, knowing the symptoms is just a small part of creating a powerful ideal client profile.

What Is the Main Problem According to Your Ideal Client?

To your ideal client, their symptoms are their problem. Let's call their symptoms a surface-level problem. Then there is a root-cause problem, which is the reason they have the symptoms in the first place.

Think about what they're typing into Google. Your ideal client doesn't know about the underlying root-cause problem causing their symptoms; to them, their symptoms—the surface-level problem—is the one they want to get rid of.

For example, your ideal client could be typing into Google something like "how to get rid of acne naturally." To your ideal client, their painful problem is acne. But we know that acne is a symptom being caused by something else. Or they could type into Google "how to sleep through the night." The problem according to your ideal client is that they're tired and can't sleep through the night. But something else is going on that is causing them to have disrupted sleep.

To help you define the problem according to your ideal client, make a list of the symptoms your ideal client would be Googling.

When it comes to creating ideal client demographics, the goal is to be able to get a clear, surface-level picture of who your ideal client is. The next part, creating the ideal client psychographics, is where the magic happens. I know that it might not be the most exciting thing and you might not have answers to the questions I'm about to ask you. But do your best to come up with answers anyway. At the end of this section I'll give you some resources that will help you better complete your profile.

Identify the Psychographics

Psychographics is data about a specific group of people that focuses on attitudes, beliefs, interests, mindsets, lifestyle, and other psychologically based criteria.

The psychographic elements that you're going to create will help you to understand what your ideal client's motivation is and why they're going to say 'yes' to working with you. Sadly, promoting the absence of symptoms isn't going to cut it. To stand out in a crowded marketplace and secure business you need to identify the client's underlying motivation. There's a reason behind the reason, so to speak, and when you know what that is, then you've found the golden ticket.

When you tackle this section, you will think that identifying the demographics was easy. Yet don't dismiss this section. The more details you give, the easier it will be for you to grow a business and get clients. Let me just say this... social media channels change, software changes, algorithms screw with your traffic, and tactics change. But the fundamentals of learning what your ideal clients want, understanding why they want it, determining what's stopping them from getting it, and learning how you can help them—and on top of that then being able to pivot based on the current landscape—is what makes your business bulletproof.

Don't skip over answering these questions. Again, it's all about laying a solid foundation from which to build. Spend time working through this section. As you gain experience, your ideal client profile will become clearer. Defining and updating your ideal client profile is an ongoing process, and you will prioritize this as your business grows. Everything you create moving forward comes from this profile. So if you don't have one, you'll feel clueless.

Why Does Your Ideal Client Want to Get Rid of the Problem?

Why do they want to get rid of the symptoms, the surface-level problem? What are their hopes, dreams, and desires? What are they hoping will happen to them, or how are they hoping they'll feel after the problem is gone?

Write out 'what', and then continuously ask yourself 'why'... 'why does it matter?' Nobody wants to lose weight just to lose weight. Sure, fitting into their cute clothes is awesome, but why does that matter to them? Why does getting rid of their IBS really matter beyond not wanting to know where every toilet is on their way to work?

How Is the Problem Affecting Their Wellbeing and Life?

In other words, how is the problem as they experience it affecting them? They're bloated and gassy... so what? They may pass up social activities, they may not want to go out in public in case they pass gas, or they may not be able to wear that new tight skirt because it won't fit by the end of the day. They have acne. So what? They have Type II diabetes. So what? Take a walk in your ideal client's shoes. Get to know how that problem is affecting their everyday life. Truly understanding and empathizing with their biggest frustrations and challenges are the most important aspects to defining your ideal client profile.

What Is Their Experience in Trying to Solve the Problem?

What have they tried before to get rid of the problem? Were they successful? For how long? Why didn't it work (from their point of view, not yours), and how did they feel when it didn't work? How much money have they already spent?

It's helpful here to list their past attempts and use as many brand names as possible. Think about the allure of those other efforts and why they didn't work.

What Are Their Biggest Fears?

You need to get dark on this one. What keeps them awake at night? What do they worry about in their mind but never say out loud? These fears are often irrational, but valid nonetheless. People are more motivated by pain than they are by pleasure. The pain and fears they have will motivate them to take action more than the idea of seeking pleasure would. Being able to address their deepest, darkest fears in your content will help you to stand out and get attention because you're addressing something that is secretly very real and scary for them.

What Are Their Hopes, Dreams, and Desires?

Can you describe a vivid picture of what life would look and feel like after working with you? Whether the outcome you're promising is a tangible thing or not, you're selling a dream, and you need to be able to clearly communicate what that dream is so that your ideal client gets inspired and excited to have it. Talking about not having the symptoms anymore isn't enough when it comes to selling the dream. What is your ideal client's biggest desire? If the pain was gone, what would be a specific scenario that they'd love to experience?

What Will Happen to Them If They Choose to Do Nothing?

If they choose to continue down the same path, what will happen to them specific to their health, mindset, and quality of life in one, three, or five years from now? What will their marriage be like? What will their pain be like? What other issues will arise? How productive will they be? How will the problem affect their career, or their relationships with their family, etc.? How will doing nothing contribute to making the problem worse?

What Phrases, Exact Language, and Vernacular Do They Use?

This might seem like a weird one, but it's important because you want to be speaking the same language as your ideal client. Call it what you want—'lingo', 'jargon', 'buzzwords'—there are definitely niche language choices and specific terms running through your ideal client's mind and being voiced when your ideal client is talking about their problem among friends and loved ones. More importantly, it's those phrases they will be punching into Google. Document how they describe their pain, hopes, and dreams. Keep a spreadsheet of words and phrases so you can use them in your content. Communicating like your ideal client will help you to stand out from the crowd.

There are resources at the end of this section to help you gather the phrases and language of your ideal client.

What Makes Them Happy?

Your ideal client is an emotional being. An often-undiscussed component of standing out from the crowd and getting clients is creating a brand that makes your audience and ideal clients feel good about themselves, whether they ever decide to work with you or not. When you know what makes your ideal client happy (think about their personality), you can add in these touchpoints throughout their prospect-to-client journey with you. Surprising, delighting, and inserting happiness into your brand can create a deeper level of emotional connection that cultivates loyal and raving clients long-term.

The End Result

Once you have completed (in as much detail as possible) the demographic and psychographic sections, you should have a well-rounded ideal client profile. You should be able to conceptualize your ideal client as one person who has a name, distinguishing features, and a defined persona.

Name your ideal client and find a photo using Google images that represents them. Then summarize your ideal client information into a comprehensive profile so that if you handed it to your ideal client, it would make them think you were an undercover CIA profiler who had been stalking them for the last year and a half.

Defining your ideal client and creating a detailed profile is one of the hardest parts of growing your business. The good news is that once you do it and get a baseline profile, everything else you create from this point on will fall into place.

Resources:

The Business of Becoming Podcast, Episodes 105 and 128.

You can find the podcast on iTunes, Google Play, Stitcher, and iHeartRadio.

Answerthepublic.com

This is an amazing and totally underutilized resource for giving you invaluable insights into what your ideal clients are thinking. You type in a keyword, and the tool generates a diagram of related searches. This tool has both a free and a paid version. It's worthwhile to make the investment.

Book Reviews

Search for books on the niche or topic your business specializes in and read the book reviews. You'll get insights into what your ideal clients are struggling with and, more specifically, the language that they use.

Facebook Groups

There are plenty of Facebook groups that you could join that have your ideal clients. It's one of the best ways to observe your ideal client and conduct research. You'll get plenty of insights, and you'll be able to probe and ask questions. Just don't be an asshole and try to poach clients from someone else's group. They worked hard to build that community and that is to be respected.

Interviews

The best way to come up with answers to the questions above is to interview people who have the symptoms you can help get rid of. The people you interview could be clients, friends, colleagues, or strangers. The point is, the best way to really understand your ideal client is to talk to them and ask them the questions I've outlined for you in the demographic and psychographic sections.

Action Steps

→ Identify with whom you most want to work.

→ Complete the demographic section.

→ Complete the psychographic section.

→ Organize your ideas and answers.

→ Create your ideal client profile.

Chapter 6

Pillar 1:
HOW TO STAND OUT FROM THE CROWD

All the way down the escalator I repeated these words: "I am smart. I deserve to be here." I was walking into a room of 500+ women all waiting to hear my talk, *The 5 Secrets to Fat Loss for Women over 45*. It was the biggest audience I had ever spoken to at that time, and I made sure to wear a black top so that my pit stains would barely show. I didn't eat that morning because I was so nervous that my already-faulty digestive system would break down just as I was about to take the stage—or worse, on stage.

It didn't matter that I had given this talk dozens of times before. This time was different because I knew what I had to lose—500 potential clients. The organizer of the conference handled registration so I couldn't collect contact information. I was being paid to talk (yay!) and therefore couldn't sell anything. But when I asked if I could give away a seven-day fat-loss meal plan specifically designed for women over 45 to all the attendees as a gift, the organizer beamed. "You'd really want to do that? That's an amazing gift. Sure, go ahead."

This was before I was 'strategic.' But I learned from the books I studied that I needed to collect contact information because having contact information meant having leads—and having leads meant having potential clients. I didn't know that what I was giving away as a gift was called a 'lead magnet.'

All I knew was that there were going to be 500 potential clients sitting in that audience, and I would be a fool not to get their contact information, which at the time was their phone number and email. Even back then I took imperfect action and did what I've always done: I acknowledged the Resistance, and did the work, even though it turned out to be a shit ton of work I wasn't expecting.

I printed out 20 sign-up forms that I had created in Word. The form had three columns: name, phone number, and email. I bought five clipboards, divided those sign-up forms among the five clipboards, and made sure I had lots of pens. At the beginning of my talk, I told them that my gift—the seven-day fat-loss meal plan specifically designed for women over 45— was my way of saying thank you for showing up and that I'd be happy to send it to anyone who wanted it. I passed around the clipboards, asked them to write their name, phone number, and email, and told them that I'd send them the plan via email. I explained that I needed their phone numbers as a backup in case something went wrong with the email so that I could ensure they received the fat loss meal plan.

The talk went better than I could have expected. Afterwards, there was a long line of women waiting to tell me how much they appreciated the specific tips I gave them. It didn't matter to them that I wasn't over 45. Want to know something funny? It's not like the tips I gave them were magical tips for women over 45 that only I knew about. I told them to eat protein with their breakfasts and explained why it mattered to their hormones. I gave them specific fat and fiber options to include with their lunches and explained how these would help them with their cravings later in the day. I told them what to eat after 8 p.m. if they were truly hungry. But what made it a home run for me was that I kept using real life examples that I knew they were experiencing—because by that point I knew my ideal client inside and out. They related to my tips because I used stories and real-life examples from my clients.

I left that evening with almost 400 names, phone numbers, and emails. The one thing I want to point out here is that I'm certain that I would not have received the same sign-up response had I offered clean eating recipes. I'm confident that the reason that over 400 women signed up to get the meal plan was because my gift was specifically positioned for them, and it solved a problem that they wanted solved.

Of course, I was over-the-moon thrilled… until I realized how long it was going to take me to individually email each person the plan, because at that point I didn't have an email marketing platform. Nowadays, I have a much more automated and leveraged way to attract my ideal client and capture their contact information that doesn't require me to manually email anyone, but I would do it again in a heartbeat if it meant I was going to get 400 leads.

What I'm describing here is the first pillar in the Health Expert Business Model. This can only be done effectively after you define your ideal client and know the problem (according to them) that they want solved. Then the content you create actually does what it's supposed to do, which is to grab their attention and draw them into your world with a desire to know more.

Pillar 1: How to Stand Out from the Crowd has two parts. After I give these to you, I'm going to break them down for you so that when it's time for you to create content and capture contact information, you won't waste time staring blankly at that blinking cursor. Creating content that attracts your ideal prospects into your world so that you can nurture them and turn them into clients is an ongoing part of your job. It's never-ending. But there is a smart and leveraged way to do it so that it doesn't feel tedious.

In order to grow your business, you need a continually growing audience of ideal prospects you can eventually convert into clients. Your audience are the people to whom you sell. And if you don't like the word 'sell', that's cool. Replace it with whatever word doesn't make you feel yucky. But if we're being honest, you are selling—and there is absolutely nothing wrong with that.

You are selling a solution to a problem that they want fixed.

You aren't swindling snake oil or magic beans (*ahem*, raspberry ketones). And if you aren't consistently growing your audience with new ideal prospects, some of whom will become clients and some of whom won't, then you're going to find it extremely hard to grow your business.

Back when I had my nutrition practice (before I had a clue what edu-taining content or a sales funnel was), I knew that I needed a way to get in front of potential clients. It didn't matter that my practice was in a busy gym, I had learned from my previous failure at the chiropractic clinic that this was not, nor would it ever be, a 'build it and they will come' situation. It was my responsibility to stand out and attract the right women's attention. It was my responsibility to ensure that my groups and 1:1 schedule were full, and I didn't want to feel like I was always on the hunt for clients. Because let's be honest, we're all too lazy to play that game.

It's so funny to me now to look back on how I grew my nutrition practice using key brand building, marketing, and sales fundamentals without even knowing what I was doing. All I knew was that I needed to build up a list of women who were interested in potentially working with me so that they were ready to commit when I ran another group or had an opening in my 1:1 calendar. I didn't want to wait until I was ready to start another group to get these women interested. I had to work at growing my prospect list and keeping these women engaged 24/7 so that I wasn't behind the eight ball when I was ready to enroll them into my program.

The two parts that make up Pillar 1: How to Stand Out from the Crowd are:

Part # 1: Create Value-Based, Edu-Taining Content
Part # 2: Have a Value-Based Lead Magnet

For this to make sense, I want you to think of your business as having a front of house and back of house. Everything that happens before a prospect becomes a client is front of house, and everything that happens after a prospect becomes a client is the back of house. Right now, your house is empty. So you need ways to get the right people (your ideal prospects) to the house so you can move them from the front to the back. This is where your value-based, edu-taining content and value-based lead magnets come into play.

Part # 1: Create Value-Based, Edu-Taining Content

So how *do* you get people to your house in the first place?

The first step is to make your ideal prospects aware that you exist. Remember that growing your business and getting clients isn't a 'build it and they will come' situation. That means that you have to insert yourself into the places where your ideal prospects already hang out so that you can capture their attention. Then you need to pique and then hold their interest by dangling a solution to their problem in front of their face.

Places your ideal prospects might be hanging out:
- Facebook
- Instagram
- YouTube

- Pinterest
- TikTok
- Associations
- Organizations
- Trade shows
- Conferences

A big mistake I see practitioners and coaches make is that they build a website and have a work-with-me page or a services page. They expect ideal prospects to just stumble upon their website, click the work-with-me page that features their services, and just buy right from the page. That used to work back in the day... it doesn't anymore. Social media and live video changed the game we're all playing.

The way to get ideal prospects to your house so that they know you exist is to consistently create value-based, edu-taining content that speaks directly to the problem that they're looking to solve. This way, when they do a Google search or scroll through any social media newsfeed, the content that you've created is right there, grabbing their attention.

As much as you might not like to hear this, I want you to think of the internet and social media as marketing platforms. For us, social media is no longer for personal use. We need to use social media as publishing platforms that deliver our message so that the ideal prospects we most want to work with can find us and connect with us. That's why it's important to consistently be publishing value-based, edu-taining content.

What is value-based, edu-taining content? Good question, I'm glad you asked, LOL.

Let me start off by telling you what it's not. Value-based, edu-taining content isn't:

- Random recipes
- Generic tips
- Irrelevant posts or pictures (think pictures of cats) that have nothing to do with the solution you offer
- Boring, scientific blog articles devoid of personality
- Straight up sales pitches for your services

Value-based, edu-taining content is content that is relatable, educational, and entertaining and yet that holds a specific intent to lead readers into your house.

That next step—or call to action (CTA) as we refer to it in the marketing world—informs the reader what you want them to do next. That next step might be to click a link, reply to an email, comment below, sign up for something, or make a purchase. The bottom line is that the value-based, edu-taining content you create and publish needs to pique the reader's curiosity and hold their attention until they feel compelled to take the next step.

You have already created your ideal client profile by identifying their psychographics and personal attributes (think back to Pillar +1: Who Do You Want to Serve?), determining the problem they want to solve, and acquiring all the other relevant information. Now it's time to take all that information and make it as sexy, exciting, and attention-grabbing as possible so that when your ideal prospect is scrolling, they feel compelled to stop and read or watch your content.

Now you're probably thinking, 'okay, I get it'. I need to consistently create content and publish it on the platforms where my ideal prospects hang out so that I can make them aware that my business exists, but what content do I create?

Again, good question. I'm going to tell you.

Over the years of working with practitioners and coaches, I've learned that the easiest way to consistently create value-based, edu-taining content is by categorizing your ideas. Then do a brainstorm for each category so that you have ongoing lists of content ideas to which you can constantly add. This way, when it comes time to create content you can easily pull ideas from the different categories.

Here are 12 value-based, edu-taining content categories for you to use:

1. **Your backstory:** This is where you tell specific 'before' stories describing how you felt before you made the discovery and the transformation, assuming you struggled with the same problem. If not, tell the backstory of why you decided to make this your career. It's helpful to brainstorm specific experiences that you had back in the day that you know your ideal client is experiencing now.

2. **Dark night of the soul:** Another way to describe this is 'your trigger moment'. What experience did you have where you decided that you were no longer going to live like this? Everyone has a moment when they decide to make a change. What was that for you?

3. **Trial and error:** After you decided that you were no longer going to live in pain, what things did you try? What worked? What didn't? How did it feel? Think about the trial-and-error situations that your ideal clients are going through so that you can create relatable content.

4. **The discovery:** This is where you describe your big 'aha!' moment—that moment when you discovered that all your attempts to fix your problem weren't working. The discovery is kinda like the root cause that nobody told you existed. Your ideal clients are trying to fix their symptoms, not the root cause, so this is where you can connect the dots for them.

5. **The transformation:** What does life look and feel like now? This is meant to be inspirational. Think about the hopes and dreams that your ideal clients have and describe some experiences that you're able to have that you couldn't before.

6. **The fundamentals:** This is content more focused on teaching and connecting the dots between symptoms and the root cause so you can help them to understand why their trial-and-error fixes aren't working. You're opening their minds to fixing the problem in a new way.

7. **Big myths, big differences:** What do they believe, or what are they doing because that's the way they've always done it—but it's wrong and unhelpful? What are some of the

little-known things that you did that made all the difference between success and failure?

8. **This changes everything:** What is something new—a new piece of information, a new way of looking at things, or a new way of doing things—that will make a difference for them? Maybe it's something that changed the game for you once you became aware of it and that will do the same for them. It's not their fault they didn't know this, but if they miss it, they won't get the results they're hoping for.

9. **If I can do it, so can you:** This is where you can outline the objections you think you're going to get. Use either your own story or case studies of clients to highlight the point that if I can do it (and I'm no different from you), then you can do it too.

10. **Us versus them:** Everyone wants to feel a part of something. Who or what can you highlight as a villain and rally support against? Who can you blame for their current situation? How can you make your ideal prospects self-identify with your community and make them want to be a part of your world?

11. **Credibility versus vulnerability:** Demonstrate through your content your knowledge and that you possess the expertise to help them. You'll share the fundamentals and give specific strategies to help them get results even before they work with you, but you don't want to come across as

perfect or unrelatable. So, in addition to positioning yourself as credible, you're also going to share vulnerable real-life moments so that you come across as just a normal imperfect person (because you are).

12. **Random fun:** This is where you can create massive engagement and have fun with your audience. Think of fun A or B questions or post memes, emojis, or GIFS based on a feeling. Talk about things that you'd chat about with your BFF (best friend forever).

The other types of content that you'll create are promotional. I didn't include these in the 12 value-based, edu-taining posts because the promotional posts have a specific intention: to get the ideal prospect to take a dedicated action that pulls them deeper into your world and leads them to having a sales conversation with you. The type of promotional content you'll include is specific to what marketing or sales campaign you're promoting.

You'll include promotional posts for the following:

- Lead magnet(s)
- Facebook group
- Webinar
- Program
- Other offers

Now here's how you use these 12 value-based, edu-taining content categories:

* Create a spreadsheet with each content category featured in its own cell running across the first row of the spreadsheet.
* Underneath each content category, referencing your ideal client profile summary that you've already created, brainstorm five to ten different experiences, ideas, or topics you could cover, and add each one to the row, moving down the spreadsheet as you add new ideas.
* Make this a running brainstorm list and use the spreadsheet to add new ideas as they come or as you get inspiration or clarity from working with your ideal client.
* Pick one to two days a month where you create several social media posts so that you're not constantly having to create content.

As ideas, thoughts, inspiration, and questions come to your mind, add them to your content spreadsheet so that when it comes time to write content you're not starting with a blank page. The practitioners and coaches we work with find it very beneficial to do this. Personally, I have a file on my phone in the notes section where I add all my content ideas. This ensures that I have a long list of subjects to write about.

Use the 3-2-1 posting schedule. I got this framework from social media guru Theresa Depasquale, founder of Capture Social Group. She suggests posting three to five times a week and running through the 3-2-1 framework on a two-week cycle:

3 posts that are personality based/edu-taining
2 posts that are fundamentals/teaching
1 post that is promotional

Here's what this would look like in practice:
- Day 1: backstory (edu-taining)
- Day 3: dark night of the soul (edu-taining)
- Day 5: fundamentals (teaching)
- Day 7: trial and error (edu-taining)
- Day 10: promotional (promotional)
- Day 12: fundamentals (teaching)
- Day 14: random fun (edu-taining)

So what you're going to do is create and publish content three to five times per week across the platforms that you know your ideal prospects are hanging out on. You can publish the same content across all the platforms. You don't need to create different content for different platforms. If you wanted to go to the trouble, you could stagger the posts so that you're not posting the same content on Facebook and Instagram simultaneously but switching up the posts or the days.

There is a purpose for consistently publishing all this value-based, edu-taining content. When your ideal prospect is searching for a solution to their problem, you stand out from the crowd and suddenly they are aware that you exist. They stop, they read or watch your content, and then they are hooked. They like you and they want to know more. Because you understand how to grow your business and get clients, your content takes them to the next step, which is to collect their contact information via your value-based lead magnet.

Part # 2: Have a Value-Based Lead Magnet

"Wait, Lori… I get that I'm supposed to publish edu-taining content on platforms where my ideal prospects already hang out so that they can become aware that I exist and so that I can help them with their problem. I get that publishing this type of content helps me to stand out from the crowd, builds my brand awareness, and helps ideal prospects to get to know me. But how do I get clients from that?"

The short answer is that you don't—not directly anyway. There are a couple of steps that need to happen between someone becoming aware that you exist and someone becoming a client. The next part in Pillar 1: How to Stand Out from the Crowd is, you guessed it… having a value-based lead magnet to capture the ideal prospect's contact information, specifically their email address.

Why their email? Because email will be the primary way you communicate, build trust, and move the prospect into a sales conversation. Social media is for creating awareness and brand-building. It's important, for sure, but there is social media etiquette that dictates that it's not to be used to 'hard sell'. It's a social platform, and if you overly promote, your engagement will go down; you don't want that. Guess where you can always promote your program or service? Email! Plus, you don't want to build your audience on someone else's land. When you only have a social media following, you don't own your audience, and it can disappear in the blink of an eye because of an algorithm change. I've had many friends and colleagues who have their account shut down, and because they didn't have an email list, their business came to a grinding halt.

The goal is twofold: to always be building up an audience on social media and then to pull them off social media and onto your email list. Then you have their attention in two places, social media and email. More attention is always better. Remember, you want to inject yourself into every place where your ideal prospect (regardless of age) already hangs out. And the two places they hang out the most are social media and email.

The truth is that the success of your business is directly linked to the size of and the *relationship* you have with your email list.

I don't have many regrets in my life, but I do regret this… I wish I had started building my email list sooner. My email list is the #1 way I generate revenue in my business. I don't have a massive social media following, nor do I really focus on growing my social media following. I focus and spend a lot of money on paid advertising to grow my email list with ideal prospects.

So how do you collect contact information so you can start to grow your email list?

What Is a Value-Based Lead Magnet?

A value-based lead magnet is a piece of content that you'll use to capture the ideal prospect's name and email address. In doing so, they are making the decision to subscribe or opt in to your email list. These days most ideal prospects don't give up their precious email address for just a plain old newsletter or to get more information about your program or service. Everyone is aware of spam, and everyone does their best to avoid it.

Having a value-based lead magnet gives them the opportunity to try you out and get a result (a win) before they ever pay money to work with you. Typically, the lead magnet is offered *for free*. But make no mistake about it: a critical transaction happens every time someone raises their hand and decides to opt in to receive your lead magnet.

This piece of content is the first exchange of value your prospect makes with your business. Sure, they've likely already engaged with your social media, but if they decide to take the next step and subscribe to get your lead magnet, then it becomes an exchange of value. The lead magnet (the content) is offering them a targeted solution to their problem, and in exchange for that, they're giving you precious space in their inbox.

That means that you want to lead with your best foot forward and deliver incredible value. You want to *wow*! them so that they want to continue to receive content from you. That content will be your emails, which continue to deliver value.

One of my guiding principles which helps to explain the purpose of the value-based, free lead magnet is from Zig

Ziglar, *"You'll get everything you want in life if you just help enough other people get what they want."* Think of your value-based lead magnet as a way for you to build goodwill before you ever even ask them for anything in return.

What Kind of Value-Based Lead Magnet Should I Create?

It should be something short and sweet so that your ideal prospects can consume the content and get a positive result quickly.

Some examples of lead magnets that are used in health businesses:

- One- or two-page PDFs: created in Word or Google docs and then saved as a PDF
- Quiz: they take a quiz and opt in to receive their results
- Checklists: 'cheat sheet,' 'swipe file,' and 'blueprints' are other fun terms being used
- Resource guides or e-books
- Toolkits or resource lists
- Mini recipe books: best to use one you've created yourself, or one that was done for you (and copyright-free)
- How-to or multi-day email courses
- Three- to five-day challenges: these are super popular and use a combination of email and social media posts to engage your audience

To create a value-based lead magnet that your ideal prospects want to receive, follow these principles:

- Make the content relevant to the problem they want to solve.
- Clearly define the result your ideal prospect is going to get.
- Make sure the content is considered valuable to your ideal prospect.
- Make sure it's quickly consumed and easy to digest.
- Make it simple yet actionable.

Here are the exact steps you need to take, in the proper order, to create your value-based lead magnet:

1. **Choose the *one* specific result that your ideal prospects want.**

Refer to your ideal client profile for this one. In their own words, what is the problem that they don't want to have anymore? Now, you're not going to give away the entire farm for free, but you do want to give them specific, actionable strategies that will get them a positive result.

For example, if the problem you're going to solve for your ideal client is to get rid of their anxiety, maybe you want to create a short morning and evening meditation audio that helps them to reduce anxiety. Here's another example: your solve is to help ease painful bowel movements for clients, you could create a three-day bowel-soothing meal plan.

2. **Create the content.**

Once you know *what* problem you're solving and you've brainstormed the actionable strategies you're going to give them, it's time to create the actual content your ideal prospects will receive in exchange for providing their email address. This is when you write the e-book, create the challenge, record the audio, etc.

It should be easy to follow and actionable. Remember that your ideal prospect is looking for a solution to their problem, and you want to give that to them to a degree; this isn't the time to delve into complex scientific topics or write a 30-page e-book describing why they have the problem in the first place.

This is where you take the path of least resistance and just create the content. It doesn't need to be fancy or professionally created. Don't worry about the length. Just create a piece of content that gives the ideal prospect strategies to get a quick win. Some of my most successful lead magnets were Word docs that I converted into PDFs.

3. **Create a dedicated opt-in page.**

Now we're getting into the tech part, which I know can feel a bit scary, but it doesn't have to be. I'm not going to get into the specifics of what tech platform to use or how to set it up. I'm going to explain the concept so that when you're ready to create your lead magnet opt-in page, you will understand what you're doing.

In order for you to capture the ideal prospect's contact information, you'll have to use an email marketing platform.

There are a variety of platforms to choose from. You can Google to get a list. You'll use the platform to create a form that the ideal prospect can fill out that then automatically subscribes them to your email list. Once they complete the form, their contact information is automatically entered, and they are now on your email list.

The form is connected to an automation that gets triggered when the person completes the form. In order to deliver the lead magnet content, you'll have to set up an email that includes the link to the lead magnet content so that the triggered automation can send the email to the new subscriber.

4. **Promote the lead magnet.**

Now that you have the lead magnet content and an opt-in page, all that's left for you to do is to promote the value-based lead magnet content to your audience. You can create content to promote the lead magnet and then publish the content on your social media platforms. Remember to use the 3-2-1 framework I went through previously.

The email marketing platform you've chosen will give you a URL to the form you've created (they all do this). You'll include a call to action (next step) in your promotional content that tells the person reading or watching to click the link to access the free guide/checklist/whatever it is that you've created. Then the ideal prospect will click the link. They'll be taken over to the opt-in page, where they will enter their name and email because they so badly want the value-based lead magnet content you've created.

BOOM! You've got yourself a new email subscriber.

Okay, so give yourself a pat on the back because now you have value-based, edu-taining content that's going to make you stand out from the crowd and attract your ideal prospect so they know you exist. In addition to that, you have a value-based lead magnet that's going to collect your ideal prospect's contact information so that you can move them to the pillar—which means you're one step closer to getting a new client. Isn't that exciting?

Action Steps

- Pick one or two social media platforms where your ideal prospects hang out so you can publish your content there.
- Follow the guidelines to create your value-based, edu-taining content and brainstorm 5-10 ideas for each of the 12 categories.
- Create a publishing schedule using the 3-2-1 framework.
- Brainstorm ideas for your value-based lead magnet.
- Create the value-based lead magnet.
- Set up your opt-in page.
- Promote the value-based lead magnet as part of your 3-2-1 content framework.

Chapter 7

Pillar 2:
THE KLT + E SEQUENCE

Nobody gets married on the first date. I say this in almost every webinar I do when I start talking about the KLT + E Sequence. Once though, someone posted in the comments, "Does getting married on the third date count?" Um…

Imagine being on a first date. The person you're with is mostly a stranger. You may have had a couple of interactions via text or phone, but this is the first time you're meeting in person. You're enjoying a lovely dinner and then *bam*… they pop the question. "Excuse me? What did you just ask me? Is this a joke? I don't even know you and you want to marry me?" Bye.

The reason why you (and 99.9% of people) don't get married on the first date is because you have no idea if the person you're sitting across is the right one for you. Maybe you're skeptical because you've dated so many other people and you're doubtful that this person is 'the one'. Or maybe you've just started playing the field and feel the need to date more before making a decision on who to marry. Or maybe you're really not even ready to get married but you just want to see who's out there.

Just like you don't pop the question on a first date because that's weird and awkward, you also don't make the 'sales ask' to a new subscriber who's just found out about you because that's salesy and pressurey (and yes, I made that word up). And now you see where I'm going with this little story, right?

At this point in the Health Expert Business Model, you are growing an audience of ideal clients via different publishing platforms like social media or podcasts or by doing free talks, and you're getting those people onto your email list via your value-based lead magnet. But before you can transition them into becoming a new client, it's important that they get to KNOW, LIKE and TRUST you first. Why? Because you don't get married on a first date!

Just because they are consuming your free content via social media and are on your email list doesn't mean that they know anything about you or really even understand how you can help them. At this point, you're still a random stranger they found on the internet, and it's your job to earn their trust before you introduce your program and explain how you can really help them.

Deciding to work with you isn't like buying a pair of jeans. Making the decision to work with you and to enroll into your program means they are committing to making changes that most likely they're afraid to make and, further, don't really want to make. I mean, let's be honest: most people don't really want to overhaul their entire lifestyle, which is what they think they'll need to do.

Am I right?

The reality is, you're likely not the first practitioner or coach with whom your ideal prospect has worked. Your program isn't the first program they've spent money on to try and fix their problem. More than likely their past includes many different attempts to get rid of their painful problem, and, as a result, they've built up a healthy dose of skepticism—ultimately a fear that whatever they try next won't work. It doesn't matter that whatever they tried before probably wasn't the right thing for them or that they are the ones truly responsible for why it didn't work. The point is, they've found you and they're skeptical. That's why this pillar of the Health Expert Business Model is so critical to turning the ideal prospect into your ideal client.

What is the KLT + E Sequence?

The KLT + E Sequence stands for: **Know, Like, Trust & Engage**, which is what you'll be doing at this stage so you can draw the new ideal prospect deeper into your world with the intention of building rapport with them and getting them to know, like, and trust you.

The KLT + E sequence is a series of three emails that gets sent automatically to new subscribers after they receive the email that delivers your value-based lead magnet content.

Think back to our dating/marriage example. Imagine going on a date with a person and having a really good time.

The date ends, and you feel really excited about the possibility of another date, but then a day goes by and there's no text or phone call when you're expecting one. Then three days go by and nothing. You've been ghosted. It's a horrible feeling not to hear from the person again, especially when you had your hopes up. Of course you could reach out, but you had expectations of being the receiver of a call or text, so you move onto the next date.

A big mistake I see practitioners and coaches often make is that they don't send any follow-up emails after they have worked so hard to get ideal prospects onto their email list. Essentially, they've gone on a first date and then ghosted the new subscriber. The new subscriber could search for ways to get in touch, but with plenty of fish in the sea, they don't bother. They return to their Google search to find someone else who can potentially help them. The moral of the story is: don't ghost your subscribers!

How to Create the KLT + E Sequence

Again, the KLT + E Sequence is a series of three emails (you can write more but start with these three) that gets delivered every two days after the lead magnet delivery email. You will write these emails and load them into your email marketing platform so that they are automatically delivered. You write them, set it, and forget it. Amazing, right?

The purpose of these emails is to better introduce yourself, your brand, and your business. You'll share your story, your discovery, and a case study. Each email will have a next step call to action so that you can start training your subscribers—right from the very beginning—to take the next step with you. Each email has a specific purpose, which I'll explain below, but the overall intention of the sequence is to build rapport, trust, and likability. As you'll see below, the engagement part comes in via the call to actions.

Email # 1: Your Story

NOTE: you can re-use the content you created for your high-value edu-taining backstory posts.

The purpose of the 'my story' email is to open up and be vulnerable with your subscribers about your backstory, which is the time in your life where you felt the exact same way as they do now. You share details about what life felt and looked like for you so that the person reading it feels like you're telling their story. Keep in mind that this email is written as a story, not as a timeline of facts.

You share your backstory as a lead up to why you now do the work that you do, because you are no longer dealing with the pain and it's now become your mission to help other people avoid the trial and error, confusion, frustration, and pain you went through. You use your backstory as a way to position your mission—who you are, who you help, and how you can help.

The 'my story' email is not a place for your professional resume or for you to vomit your entire life story onto the page. You share a specific moment in time that you experienced before you went through the transformation. The moment in time should be relatable to an experience that you know your ideal prospects are dealing with now so that they feel like you understand what they're going through.

Now, if you don't have a personal story, that's okay. Think back to why you wanted this career in the first place. What motivated you? Or you can use a client's experience to illustrate that you understand where they are and the pain they are going through, and then relate it to your mission, who you help, why, and how.

You want this email to lead into the next, so you pique their interest by alluding to that next email where you'll be telling them the discovery you made that changed everything for you. This way they'll be looking forward to getting the next email from you.

At the end of the email, add in the call to action. That's the engagement part. You want your subscribers to take the action, which is to reply to your email. This opens up the opportunity for you to engage with them in real time.

A call to action at the end of this email could be worded like this:

PS: Hit reply and let me know the #1 thing you're struggling with when it comes to [whatever it is they're trying to get rid of].

Then you end the email with your signature.

Then two days later the second KLT + E sequence email goes out automatically (because you scheduled it that way). This email is the discovery email.

Email # 2: The Discovery

NOTE: you can *still* re-use the content you created for your high-value, edu-taining discovery posts.

The purpose of the discovery email is to show your subscribers the big root cause they are unaware of, how making this discovery changed everything for you, and how making this discovery is now the cornerstone of the work you do with your clients. Even if you don't have any clients yet, that's okay. It will become the work you do with your clients.

You can include the trial-and-error attempts you went through and describe how you felt. The purpose is to demonstrate that you've tried the same or similar things that they're trying now. Make sure that you're vulnerable here and explain how it felt for you—share your frustration, anger, sadness, embarrassment, etc. You want to relate to the current experiences of your ideal prospects.

Then you describe the big discovery, which is either the root cause or the feature that turned everything around for you. For example, maybe you discovered that unbalanced blood sugar was causing those uncontrollable cravings, serious gut issues were causing your acne, or food sensitivities were causing your migraines.

At this point you can introduce a piece of new information as a potential reason for why everything that they've been trying hasn't worked. What you don't do is tell them what to do to fix it—that's what they will pay you for. The discovery is the missing piece of the puzzle that, once you found it, led to your transformation.

In this email you allude to the next email by telling them

that you're going to share how X client got rid of/beat/fixed [whatever the problem] was and that you'll be spilling the secrets so that they can see that getting rid of/beating/fixing [whatever the problem is] is possible for them too.

You can end the email with a call to action like this:

"Do me a favor, hit reply and let me know one thing you'd love to experience after you get rid of [whatever the problem is]."

Then close the email with your signature.

Two days later the third and final KLT + E sequence email goes out automatically (because you scheduled it that way). This email is the case study email.

Email # 3: The Case Study Email

NOTE: There isn't a case study category in the high-value edu-taining content list, but you can definitely add it.

This email is a bit tricky because, depending on where you are in your business-building journey, you might not have any client case studies yet. That is totally okay. Here's what I want you to do: think about a friend or loved one that you helped. Can you use them as a case study? If not, maybe use yourself.

The purpose of this email is to share a case study in the form of a story that details a before-and-after transformation. As you share the before-and-after transformation, you're sharing details of the client's (or your) mindset. You want to include how they were feeling before they started to work with you. (I'm using the term 'work' loosely here. Whether they paid you or not doesn't matter.)

You want to describe why they wanted to work with you (their hopes and dreams), why they were hesitant to get started (blocks/objections), what some of the reasons were why they didn't think it would work (past experiences), how they felt during the process (positive changes), and then the big transformation (desired outcome), which describes how they feel now.

The point is to have the subscriber see themselves in the case study and to elicit hope that if this person can do it, so can they. Leave them feeling inspired and curious about what it would be like for them to work with you too.

This email also positions you as an expert. It demonstrates that you're able to help someone who is just like them. Since this is the last email in the sequence, you don't allude to the next one. The next email they get will be a general marketing email that you'll start sending out one to two times per week. I will talk about this more in Pillar 3: Getting the YES!

You can end this email with a call to action like this:

"Hit reply and respond with 'I'm Ready!' if you're ready to get rid of [whatever the problem is]."

These replies are the most important ones because what the subscriber is telling you is that they're ready, obviously, which gives you an opening to move them into the next pillar of the Health Expert Business Model.

By now I hope you can see why Pillar +1: Who Do You Want to Serve? and why creating your ideal client profile are critical to you being able to complete the remaining pillars in the Health Expert Business Model. If you didn't gather the information for your ideal client profile, you're going to have a hard time creating Pillar 1: How to Stand Out from the Crowd and Pillar 2: The KLT + E Sequence.

It's worth saying here that if you're still reading, then it's possible that you're starting to feel a little bit out of your element or perhaps even slightly overwhelmed. That's okay. Remember that you are going to take imperfect action, which in this case is to just create the content to the best of your ability. Done is always better than perfect. Try not to overthink it and/or tweak it until you think it's perfect. Think of this content as a first draft that you can come back to and improve upon when you have more information. Waiting until you feel ready is not a good idea—I promise you that such a time will never come. There is no reason, even if you don't have client experience, even if you've never created your own content before, that you can't start with Pillars +1, 1, and 2 right now. It's important for you to start putting yourself out there and growing your audience so that by the time you're done with Pillar 3: Getting the YES! and Pillar 4: Build the Methodology (The Signature Program), you've got an audience, meaning an email list of ideal prospects ready to work with you.

So take a deep breath and just start, okay?

Action Steps

- Write the three KLT emails.
- Schedule them to get sent out after your lead magnet delivery email.

Chapter 8

Pillar 3:
GETTING THE YES!

We were standing in the kitchen. Bryan, my then-husband, was standing behind the island while I was sitting on a bar stool in front. The island was the barrier between us. I was trying to explain to him why I didn't feel comfortable pushing the program so often. I wasn't doing a very good job of explaining it, though. How do you articulate your fear of coming across as too salesy or pushy? All I kept saying was that it didn't feel good to me to be constantly hounding my community to buy. It just didn't feel good. It felt uncomfortable. I didn't want anyone to think that all I cared about was making money—because I didn't! My mission was to give value, not to hard sell. It just didn't feel good…

I was crying because I felt forced to defend myself and that he just wasn't getting it. But how could he? He wasn't the one pushing the sales. He wasn't the one interacting with my audience I had worked so hard to build. He got to stay behind the scenes. I kept saying, "You just don't understand, you just don't understand."

He took a deep breath in, stood up tall, looked me in the eye, and said, "Get over yourself and this bullshit belief that selling is bad. If they don't work with you, will they ever get the result they want? No, they won't. They're going to stay stuck. And that means you've failed them. So go to whatever therapy or energy healer you need to but do yourself, and more importantly your entire community, a favor and get over it fast."

My first response came directly from my ego... "Fuck you Bryan. You don't understand!" Then, after my ego calmed down, I was truly heard what he was saying. And it was loud and clear. If my potential clients don't work with me, they're going to stay stuck—that means I've failed them. And then I went and booked a therapy appointment because I realized that the issue that I had with selling wasn't an actual truth. There was no evidence of it being true. It was a belief that I was carrying around, and it was no longer serving me, so it was time to get rid of it and replace it with a powerful new one that served both me and my community.

Pillar 3: Getting the YES! is about sales. I'm not going to pretend it's anything else by giving it a new name because that would be feeding into the bullshit lie that selling is bad. I'm not going to call it 'abundant conversations' or 'empowered enrollment' or anything like that. I used to call this part 'invitation into transformation'. And to a degree it is—you are inviting them into a transformation via your sales conversation. But let me be clear, this pillar of the Health Expert Business Model is about *sales*. It's about bringing the ideal prospect to a point where they are ready to have a *sales conversation* with you—to be clearer, to *spend money*. It's about giving you the structure and sales framework so that you can have an authoritative, confident sales conversation with your ideal prospects that ends in them saying 'YES!' to working with you.

Let's address the many sales elephants in the room before I dive into this pillar. I've been working with practitioners and coaches since 2011, most of whom are female. It doesn't seem to matter what their professional designation is, although age does seem to make a difference. Those under 40 don't seem to hold the same beliefs around charging their worth and making sales as those over 40, which is both interesting and awesome.

Let me share some of my false beliefs about sales to help you identify yours so that you can start to do the work to replace your false beliefs with ones that are supportive, positive, and empowering.

False Belief # 1: I Don't Want People to Think That All I Care About Is Making Money

The fear was that if I promote, promote, promote and sell, sell, sell to people, my community and people watching me would think: "This is all about the money. If she was really invested in helping us grow our businesses, then she wouldn't charge so much, and she'd do more stuff for free." So I held back on increasing my prices for business coaching for a long time, and I barely promoted my services. That led to me feeling stressed out because we weren't able to make our revenue goals, which meant that a) I wasn't really helping my clients and b) because of the financial stress, I wasn't able to show up as the confident, empowered mentor I so badly wanted to be.

False Belief # 2: My Audience Won't/Can't Pay What I'm Asking

This was a big one for me when I had my nutrition practice because I was working with women who were used to Weight Watchers, which at the time was $17 per month. I wrongly believed that there was no way they would pay me $997. Well, they did! And without objection.

This false belief has crept in many times since then. And every time it does, I'm shown an example of it not being true. I've put out programs where the investment has been $7, $97, $997, or $10,000, and for all those fees there have been objections—and there have also been people who have either found the money or had it to invest without objection.

I've learned over the years that it's not my decision whether or not someone will or won't, can or can't pay the fee I'm asking. My responsibility is to assign a fee that enables me to provide the best quality service for my clients.

False Belief # 3: I Don't Have Enough Experience to Charge a High Fee

When I started offering 1:1 business coaching services, I charged $97 per hour. Yup, less than $100 per hour to access the experience, strategies, and framework that had helped me to grow my nutrition business to multi six figures, nine locations, and 24 licensed practitioners across Canada. Freaking 97 dollars an hour. I'm literally cringing as I type that number. My rationale was, "Who do I think I am?" I couldn't possibly charge more than that because I wasn't really a business coach. I had no on-paper qualifications, and all I was doing was sharing what worked for me, so how dare I charge hundreds or thousands? If I could go back in time, I'd slap myself across the face. No wonder Bryan was so pissed at me... he could see my worth even when I couldn't.

What I've come to understand after having worked with thousands of clients over the years is that the more skin in the game the clients have (meaning the greater their investment), the more committed they are to work toward getting the result they desire. Also, my lack of on-paper credentials doesn't mean anything. People are paying for my personal experience and my ability to get them results.

False Belief # 4: I Hope That One Day I Can Afford...

This isn't so much a false belief so much as it is a lack of belief. When you live paycheck-to-paycheck for too long, you start to lose faith that there will come a day when it won't be like that. Even when my nutrition business was making money, there wasn't an abundance of it left over each month, so I never felt financially secure. I can remember journaling the day that I was: "I am debt-free and financially secure." My point for this one is that I understand that it's hard to sell from a place of integrity and service when you're financially strapped and stressed out. It's hard not to feel desperate for the sale when you are desperate for the money.

But that doesn't mean that it will be like that forever. As long as you continue to progress and as long as you continue to take imperfect action and don't quit, you will get to experience the benefits of all your hard work.

False Belief # 5: I Don't Want to Come across as Ostentatious

This one started to creep up a couple of years ago when I started to have an excess of funds available. Truth be told, I've used a cleaning service for years. But when I would casually joke about how my goal in life was to outsource all the domestic tasks so that I would never again have to grocery shop, prep, cook, clean-up, do laundry, organize my house, get the mail, change my tires, or deal with house stuff, a girlfriend I was chatting with said, "OMG, you're so high maintenance." And that activated me. I got defensive and embarrassed. It wasn't until I was in a room with people more successful than me who couldn't believe I didn't have a house manager (yup, that's a thing) that I realized that it's all just a matter of perspective.

There's one more false belief that I want to address. While I, personally, have never experienced this one, I see it blocking so many of the practitioners and coaches I work with that it would be irresponsible of me not to include it here.

False Belief # 6: I Don't Believe I Can Be Successful

While this one isn't specific to sales, I'm including it here because it's intimately tied to your ability to grow your business and get clients. Whether you believe this simply because you've never really thought about how successful you want to be, because you want to be successful but don't know how, because you've never given any thought to a dollar figure you want to make, or because you (and this might sting a bit) don't really think you have what it takes, the idea that it's not possible for you (but it is for other people) is a negative belief that simply isn't true. Just because you don't know 'the how' doesn't mean it's not possible. Everyone who has ever created something impactful begins at square one.

I'm sure you have plenty of false beliefs around asking for the sale and making money, but I'm sure of this: *those beliefs only serve to keep you stuck and playing small.*

I can give you all the strategies and frameworks, scripts, and tips in the world, but they won't matter if you're holding onto some or all the false beliefs I mentioned above. I want you to notice your beliefs around sales, making money, and success. This is important because you need to be aware of these false beliefs so that you can do the work to overthrow them. Yes, maybe you don't feel comfortable charging a high fee and asking for the sale, but why don't you? And wouldn't it feel better if you did?

Find a quiet, safe space and ask yourself these questions:
- How does promoting my business make me feel?
- How does promoting my program make me feel?

- How does charging a fee that is above average make me feel?
- How does asking for the sale and holding space to overcome objections make me feel?
- How does making more money than anyone I know make me feel?

It's helpful for you to journal these feelings. Identify them. Sit with them. Feel them. Let them feel really uncomfortable in your body. Let your mind run away with these feelings.

Now for each question, I want you to ask yourself:

- Why do I feel the way that I feel?
- What assumption or belief am I holding that might cause me to feel this way?

A warning: doing this introspective work might bring up some thoughts and feelings that activate you, and you might want help processing through them. If that's the case, I highly recommend you seek the professional services of a life coach or therapist who has experience in helping people achieve self-worth and feelings of deservingness. I am a huge advocate for therapy… there is no shame in my therapy game! I am here to become the best possible version of myself that I can be; in order to do that, I need to become aware of beliefs that aren't actually serving me—that have been imposed on me either because of cultural norms or because I let myself believe them. And if I can process through my false beliefs, so can you.

So now that we've exposed the elephants in the room, let's

move into the part where I give you the sales structure and framework that's a part of the Health Expert Business Model so that you can feel good about promoting your program and asking for the sale.

At the end of the day, you can't transform anyone's life until they become a client. Sure, the free front-of-house, high-value, edu-taining content you publish should give them small wins, but we both know that if your ideal client could use free information to get rid of their painful problem, then they would have already, and they wouldn't be in your world looking for help. They are in your world because they haven't been able to get the results that they desire, and so it's your professional responsibility to offer your program to them.

You can't truly help someone until they become a client, and the best way we've found to turn an ideal prospect into an ideal client is via a 1:1 sales conversation. Now the idea that you're going to have to sell to someone face-to-face or over the phone or via Skype or Zoom might make you cringe, but let's ignore that response for the duration of this pillar because after doing about a dozen or so calls, that vanishes.

Throughout my career as a registered holistic nutritionist and now as a business mentor, I've studied sales and have sold millions of dollars' worth of programs and services—so I've learned a lot from my work in the trenches. Although the tactics for conducting sales conversations have changed over the years, the fundamentals of how to take an ideal prospect and turn them into an ideal client haven't. What I'm about to show you works for us and most definitely works for all the practitioners and coaches that we work with. It doesn't matter what their professional designation is or what their price point is or what niche they specialize in... they all successfully follow the same framework that I'm going to give to you, the framework that will guide you through creating a structured sales process so that you can feel like a confident sales badass.

You've Got to Sell Like a Doctor

A big mistake that I see practitioners and coaches make when they try to sell their program or service is that they focus on explaining the features of the program. They try to convince the ideal prospects that they have the best 12-week program and that the modules, PDFs, and Facebook group are what will get the prospects the results they desire.

And it doesn't work.

The practitioner or coach is left feeling like a used car salesman, and they don't understand why they can't get clients. They wrongly assume it has something to do with the quality of their program, so they scrap months' worth of work and start all over again. Then the sales cycle repeats itself because they are using the same tactics that didn't work last time to try to sell their new program.

Imagine going to a doctor's appointment because you have pain, and the doctor doesn't ask you any questions about the pain. All he does is poke and prod. Then he tries to convince you that you need a certain prescription, proceeds to tell you about all the features for that pill, and then asks you if you want it.

I'm pretty sure that your response would be, "Well... I'll

have to think about it." Then you'd leave the office and seek out another opinion.

In the medical profession, *a prescription without proper diagnosis is malpractice.*

And it's the same in sales.

Once you have an ideal prospect raising their hand to identify themselves as interested and they've subscribed to your value-based lead magnet and are responding to your KLT + E sequence, the next step in the model is to motivate them to schedule a call to speak with you. Only then is it time for you to make a 'diagnosis' and give your prescription—aka, ask for the sale.

Getting the YES! is about taking your ideal prospects from a less desirable 'before' state to a more desirable 'after' state. If you can't clearly and confidently communicate that what you're offering can do that then they'll likely object, and you'll lose them as a new client.

Instead of spending most of the call on getting the ideal prospect to tell you all their symptoms and then trying to explain the features of the program as the magic pill that will fix them—hoping that the features alone will spark enough excitement that the ideal prospect will whip out their credit card—focus on 'diagnosing' the issue and then, *if the program you have can help them,* extend an invitation to work with you.

You want to shift the sales conversation away from symptoms and features because not everyone who opts for a call with you will be a good fit. The sales conversation is used to determine *if* the ideal prospect would actually be a good ideal client fit. You will have a percentage of calls where the ideal prospect is *not* a good fit, and in that case, you tell them straight out. You don't take them on as a client because that would be in neither of your best interests, even if you are desperate for the money.

There are several reasons why an ideal prospect isn't a good fit to become an ideal client:

- They don't have the problem your program solves, in which case you can't actually help them.
- They have a more intense or more difficult problem that would require you to practice outside of your scope, and therefore it would be irresponsible of you to take them on.
- Their personality isn't a right fit to work with (no amount of money is worth the hassle of dealing with someone who is aggressive, mean, or has a victim mentality).

Not only is referring them to someone else the right thing to do, but it also preserves your integrity, creates standards in your community, and creates goodwill if ideal prospects understand that you're not here to work with anyone and everyone just to make a sale.

It's a very different way of selling than the way most people are taught, but it is essential. Your structured sales process has to *clearly* position and establish in the minds of your potential client that the call with you as a 'must-have conversation' to determine *if* the program you offer is a good fit and that only after you've had the conversation will you be able to determine *if* you can help them.

I want to talk about something that isn't often talked about when it comes to sales, and that is your energetic state. Yeah, I'm going to get a bit 'woo-woo' here, but it's a real thing and it matters. Whether you conduct the sales call in person or via the phone or an online platform, the ideal prospect on the other end of the call can feel your energetic state. If you show up all nervous and unsure of yourself, they can feel that. If you show up desperate for the sale, they can feel that too.

Imagine walking into a doctor's appointment and the doctor appears to be lacking confidence. They're looking down, their tone of voice is soft, they go back and forth with their questions, and it's obvious they don't have command of the appointment. That type of demeanor doesn't instill confidence, right? Even if they give you a diagnosis and recommend a course of treatment, you're unlikely to trust their recommendations simply because of their lack of authority and certainty.

When ideal prospects show up to a call, they are expecting you to be the expert. They are expecting you to be the authority and to lead the conversation. They're expecting you to ask clear and concise questions. They're expecting you to tell them how you can help them. So it's important for you to show up in the way that they expect, whether you're feeling that way at the moment or not. This means that you need to figure out a way to shift your energetic state so that you show up as the expert and conduct the conversation with confidence and authority. I learned a long time ago that the person with the most certainty wins. That needs to be you!

"Okay, Lori, I get it. I need to have a structured sales

process in place, and it's obvious that I need to learn how to conduct a sales conversation and to feel confident while I do it, but how?" Another good question, my friend!

12 Steps to Getting the YES!

At this point in the Health Expert Business Model, you've stood out from the crowd and your ideal prospect is aware that you exist. They've gone from consuming your front-of-house high-value, edu-taining content to taking the next step, subscribing to your value-based lead magnet. They've received your KLT + E email sequence, where you've built rapport and trust. Now let's walk through the practical application of creating a structured sales process and holding a sales conversation. We do this by digging into the 12 Steps to Getting the Yes!

The 12 Steps to Getting the Yes! are:
1. Promote the Call
2. Optimize Your Mindset
3. Build Rapport
4. Investigate
5. Explain the Agenda
6. Discover the Problem
7. Connect the Implications
8. Determine the Desired Transformation
9. Review the Conversation
10. Make the Ask
11. Handle Objections/Questions
12. Proceed with Enrollment

Now it's time to motivate them to take the first step with you, which is to schedule a time to speak with you. Okay, let's get started.

Step 1. Promote the Call

In order to get ideal prospects on a call with you, they have to know that the option exists. That means that you consistently need to promote the opportunity to schedule a time to talk with you. Now, we don't want to just come right out and promote: "Hey! Got this problem? Book a call and let's chat." That's salesy and it doesn't work.

Instead, use the 3-2-1 framework I explained in Chapter 6 to create high-value, edu-taining posts where you tell a story and include a call to action that offers them the opportunity to chat with you.

You should promote the opportunity for your ideal prospects to learn more about how you can help them by publishing content on platforms like these:

- Weekly emails
- Social media
- Facebook groups
- Private message on Facebook
- Direct message on Instagram
- Facebook or Instagram Lives

The truth is, teaching you how to create content that markets and promotes the opportunity to have a call with you could be an entire book in and of itself. The goal is to show up consistently, which you'll be doing via your high-value, edu-taining front-of-house content, and to include a call to action that tells the person to click the link to schedule a call with you.

You're going to have to test out different pieces of content to see which themes work best to get calls booked. This will be an ongoing priority on your to-do list. Over time, you'll know what pieces of content are the most effective to get calls booked.

Congratulations! Now that you've booked a call, let's look at some ways to optimize your mindset.

Step 2. Optimize Your Mindset

Before we deal with mindset, I want to clear up a common misconception. An initial intake or assessment isn't the same thing as a sales conversation. Doing an initial intake happens after the ideal prospect has become an ideal client.

There's something I want you to think about. Are you having the sales conversation to make the sale because you need money or because you are truly advocating for the person's best interests? If you're truly there to serve that person, to ensure that they get the help that they desire—which might require you to refer them to someone else—then the focus should be on that instead of worrying about all the things you're likely worrying about.

Let me ask you this: how are you setting yourself up for success before the call even happens? Do you have a way to optimize your mindset and energy, to get yourself into the right frame of mind prior to the call?

Do you have cues that help you transition your energetic state into one of leadership and authority? Are you able to hold the expert frame all the way through the call? Here's something to think about… you are not on the call to be their friend or to enable them. You are not their equal. You are in a power position. You are in a position of authority, and it's important to hold that frame all the way through the call.

That doesn't mean that you have to be cold or mean. It means that you should show up as the expert—a confident leader ready to transform a person's life—and be that person throughout the call.

Having a successful call means so much more than just getting a new client. Every single person who books a call with you, whether they show up or not, is asking for help. They've booked a call because they are in pain of some kind. They are having an issue that is important enough that it motivated them to book a call, and that deserves compassion and regard.

It's your professional responsibility to create an environment to facilitate a successful call. This starts with you before the call even begins.

Let's look at some tips for creating a helpful pre-call mindset.

Helpful Pre-Call Tips:

- ✦ Change your state to get into alpha mode so you show up with confidence, certainty, and authority (it helps to listen to a song that makes you feel like you can run through walls — mine is Diva by Beyonce).

- Research the person to find out one to two personal details about them to refer to so you can build rapport (Google, Facebook, Instagram).
- Use affirmations and positive self-talk (you've got to psych yourself up - don't be afraid to say out loud 'I am the expert and they need my help' five times even if you feel silly about it).
- Have a ritual that allows you to remove *the ego* and disconnect from your goal of securing the 'YES!' so that you can be present and serve the person with integrity.
- Remind yourself that this is a real person who is looking to you for support, validation, and guidance, and who is looking for you to hold them to a higher standard than they can hold for themselves right now.
- *Mantra:* They need me; I'm exactly what they are looking for; I am here to serve them and have their highest potential in mind.
- Make sure that you are in a quiet room with no interruptions.
- Use your phone with headphones so that your hands are free for taking notes and gesticulating.
- Make sure that you are recording the phone call so you can go back and critique yourself.
- Have a pen and notepad in front of you so that you can take notes using their exact words.

- Be prepared to refer them to another program that would be a better fit if they're not a right fit for your program.
- Have the number ready to dial; make sure you dial the very moment the clock hits the minute the call is booked for.
- Be present, empathize, and listen.

Now that you're ready for the call, let's move on to the next step, which is to build rapport.

Step 3. Build Rapport

In this step, you are actively conversing with the ideal prospect. The outcome of the rapport step is to build trust and respect. When you skip building rapport and jump right to investigating, the person won't feel comfortable telling you their truth. They won't feel like they're in a safe environment to let their guard down.

There's a difference between building rapport and investigating, but you can build rapport while you investigate. Building rapport includes calling them by their name, relating to them, connecting with them, being vulnerable first by sharing a personal story, and matching their energy. You're matching their energy and sharing a personal story, which builds trust.

Step 4. Investigate

Investigating is finding out the facts. It's getting context about the situation, which is important. This is where you literally investigate, you fact-find. It's very situational and shouldn't last long.

Let's pretend I specialize in energy management and stress. Investigating sounds like this...

> **HP:** "So Jane, in preparation for this session, I was doing a little digging... I noticed on your Facebook page that you have grandchildren. How many?" [Wait for response.]

> **HP:** "Amazing. My grandmother was one of my favorite people. She was 91 when she passed. She was such an inspiration to me. I'm sure your grandchildren love spending time with you. Is that one of the reasons you wanted to chat today, so you could figure out how to have the energy to stay healthy and keep up with them?"

> **HP:** "Honestly, this is my purpose in life—to help my clients implement simple yet super-effective strategies to feel better so they can fully participate in life. Have you ever worked with a nutritionist before? Would you be open to sharing with me what made you want to do something about this now?" [Wait for response.]

> **HP:** "Thank you! Okay, amazing..."

When you combine the build rapport and the investigate stages, it becomes very powerful because you're asking them to talk about themselves and you're relating to them. So let me break down what I did during the build rapport and investigate stages…

I started the conversation by getting the ideal prospect to talk about an area of her life that she loves. This has nothing to do with her health or the reason she booked a call, so immediately her defenses went down. I got her to talk about her grandchildren, which I knew she had because I had snooped on her Facebook page. I prepared ahead of time.

Almost everyone you're going to talk to is Googleable. And if not, ask the question:

HP: "Before we begin, I'd like to share a bit about myself so you can get to know me better. I have a dog and two kids. My dog's name is X. Do you have any pets? [Wait for response.] No? What about kids?" [Ask them questions about themselves.]

So I got the ideal prospect to let her guard down by getting her to talk about an area of her life she loves. Then I related to her by sharing about my grandmother.

Then I made an assumption. Because I specialize in energy management and stress, my clients would be coming to me to get rid of their fatigue and to increase energy; so it's a pretty solid assumption that playing with her grandchildren makes her tired and that she wants more energy to keep up with them. That's a surface-level desire.

Then I shared about what I do and how important it is to me. I then asked, almost in the same sentence, if she's ever worked with a nutritionist before. She'll respond yes or no, and then I'll ask her why she wants to make a change now. That's her trigger moment. That moment is super important to identify because it's the very thing that got her to book a call. It's powerful, and you should know what it is.

You have investigated the ideal prospect's current situation (and hopefully uncovered why the call was booked), and you have built rapport. Now it's time to move to the agenda step, which outlines the phases of the call and sets its pace. It's helpful to have an agenda so when the ideal prospect goes off on a tangent or starts asking you a lot of questions, you can refocus attention back to the agreed-upon agenda for the call.

Step 5. Explain the Agenda

The agenda step is quick. Outline the different phases of the call, ensure the ideal prospect agrees with the agenda, and then with their approval, move on.

Setting the agenda also helps you to establish and maintain the leadership and authority frame. You are setting out and guiding the path.

It could sound something like this:

> **HP:** "So we only have about 45 minutes, and I want to be respectful of that. And I'd love to see how I can help you today, but in order to do that I need a bit more clarity. I'm going to start by asking a couple of

questions to get a better idea of where you're at and where you want to be, so I can determine how to best get you there in the shortest amount of time possible. And, of course, if that's something I can help you with, I'll let you know. If not, I'll definitely refer you to someone who can, so no matter what, I'll make sure you have the next- best steps."

HP: "Does this sound good? Great. You okay to dive in? Awesome."

The next step is focused on discovering the ideal prospect's problem. This is a need-to-know. They've booked a call with you because they have a problem they want to get rid of. Avoid assuming that you know what their problem is. You might know the root-cause problem that is the culprit behind their symptoms, but you need them to tell you what the problem is through their framework of understanding—as they experience it.

Step 6. Discover the Problem

This is where you dig to identify their surface-level and deep-level problems. The surface-level problem is the first thing they'll tell you about: I don't have energy; I can't lose weight; I have period pains.

But those are symptoms. *What you need to discover is why those symptoms are a problem for them.* It's the 'why' behind the symptoms that they are paying to fix. This is another big mistake I see most practitioners and coaches making... they stop digging once they have the symptoms. Sure, the symptoms are annoying and painful, but given that they've likely lived with them for so long, why are they only now wanting to fix them?

You want to discover how the symptoms are decreasing their quality of life. What are they not able to have or do because of those symptoms? And why does that matter to them?

Here's something to think about... people don't buy their way *into* something; they buy their way *out* of a problem. Most people don't buy into upgrading the roof of their house; but if they've got a torrent of rainwater coming through a leak they'll jump to buy the repair work to fix it. So what problem are they buying their way out of?

This is also where you need to hold that leadership frame and use probing questions to go from surface-level problems to identifying the deep-level problems. See, people will instinctively stay surface-level and defend their problem. They'll try to justify why they have it, but that isn't the same as digging to find out why their pain matters to them.

The goal of this section is to identify the deep-level problem that is the real motivator behind them wanting to make a change. *Find out what the problem is, and then find out why it matters.*

A good starter question would be:

HP: "So tell me, what's going on for you right now?"

A follow-up question could be:

HP: "So, what's not working for you right now?"

And you'll get a surface-level answer like, "I'm so tired all the time."

Once you know the surface-level answer, you need to probe deeper.

One of my favorite probing questions is: "Why does that matter?"

Let's continue with our pretend ideal prospect who is super tired. A probing question could be something like this:

HP: "Okay, so you're tired all the time [that's surface-level]. Why does that matter?"

They'll likely respond with something surface-level like they're missing out on fun things.

HP: "What fun things? Why does missing out matter to you? Have you been tired for a while, like more than six months? Yes, so then why do you want to have more energy now?"

If you're having trouble getting to the deep-level problem, you could ask probing questions in a different way, something like:

HP: "What would change for you if you weren't tired?"

You're likely to get the same response...

IP: "I wouldn't miss out on fun things."

Then you ask:

HP: "What fun things do you not want to miss out on? Why are those important to you?"

Then, if you've built a rapport with them, they'll tell you. The fact that they don't feel those things now is likely the deep-level problem. And then you paraphrase what they told you back to them to help them feel validated.

HP: "How would you feel if you weren't experiencing [whatever they told you] now?"

The goal of this section is to discover the deep-level problem. You'll know when you've hit on it because something shifts. It could be a shift in energy or a change in their voice, but something shifts.

The information you gather here will be used toward the end of the sales conversation. You're going to remind them why getting started now is critical: so they can have the experiences or feelings they're missing out on now and so badly want to have.

Okay, so now that you've identified both the surface-level

and deep-level problems, let's take it to the next step, which is the Connect the Implications section.

Step 7. Connect the Implications

This section is very powerful, and it comes right after you discover the problem according to the ideal prospect. You want to connect their problem with the implications of that problem. In other words, what happens if they do nothing or if the problem gets worse? Or what happens if they solve the problem—what do they get that they've never had before?

What are the implications of having this problem, as in their relationships—personally, emotionally, financially, and professionally? How will their quality of life deteriorate or improve? What will they miss out on? What will they not get that they really want? Can they afford to continue on the way they are right now? What will they get that they really want?

It's one thing to be able to discuss the deep-level problem, but when you can connect it to quality of life, then you're really onto something. Helping the ideal prospect see the truth about what the symptoms or problem are doing—how much of an impact they are truly having—is hard. It's uncomfortable and creates tension.

This is good. You want to hold that tension. Even though the ideal prospect is in pain, they've lived with that pain for a while. But feeling uncomfortable and feeling the tension will cause them to want to act to alleviate the tension, which means they're moving to a place of readiness to commit to a solution, which would be to work with you.

Being able to hold space for a person in this way is the most compassionate and supportive thing you can do. Letting the person feel the tension without breaking the framework of the conversation is powerful.

A great probing question to identify implications would be something like this:

HP: "So you're tired all the time, [paraphrase why that deeply matters to them]... has this started to affect [your relationship, time with loved ones, life experiences, etc.] yet?"

Then the ideal prospect will answer, and your response will be:

HP: "That's a big deal. That would be awful."

You don't coach. You don't try to fix the situation. You just sit there and listen and stay silent, for longer than what feels comfortable. It's your job to get the ideal prospect to feel the gravity and importance of their problem.

The ideal prospect has likely spent such a long time rationalizing their issues and having other people enable them or appease them. And here you are holding a mirror to their face and highlighting how big their problem really is without letting them off the hook.

The truth is, the person is in conversation with you because they want your help, but they're likely scared to make a change.

It's important to get them to a place where the pain of staying the same is stronger than the pain of changing.

Okay, so now that you've discovered their deep problem and the implications of having this problem, you want to shift into the positive and get them to tell you what their desired transformation would be.

The transition would look something like this:

> **HP:** "So, tell me what solving this problem looks like for you. If you weren't so tired all the time, what is one thing you'd love to do that would light you up?"

Now we are entering the Determine the Desired Transformation section.

Step 8. Determine the Desired Transformation

This is where you get the ideal prospect to tell you what they want, what they desire, and where they'd like to be once the problem is gone.

> **IP:** "When I lose X pounds, I'll feel Y, I'll do Z." "When I have clear skin, I'll be able to do X or feel Y or go to Z places."

Here's an example of how you'd do that:

HP: "Okay, so we know that you're tired [the problem] and that feeling tired sucks because [list the implications you've already discussed], so let's say we're having this conversation again six months from now, and let's say I've shown you how to get your energy back [desired outcome] so that you don't feel tired anymore. What would your day-to-day life look and feel like?"

What you're doing is summarizing the problem as they've described it, you're connecting the problem to the implications, and you're seeding that you have the strategies to solve the problem—you're asking the prospect to future pace, to put themselves in a state where they can envision the problem being gone, and to describe what that looks and feels like for them.

That's the transformation. Remember, they're paying to buy themselves out of pain, but they also want the emotional payoff of the desired outcome.

You'll also use probing questions in this section too...

HP: "Why is having [desired outcome] important? How will it make you feel to have [desired outcome]?"

HP: "If you had [list steps that will take away the pain], describe a perfect day."

The more details you can collect in this section, the better, because you'll use them again in the review section.

Let's pause for a moment here and go through what we've covered so far, because the next step is the review step; here you'll review but also compare and contrast where they are now with where they want to be, and elucidate the gap that lies between the two.

We started with adjusting and optimizing your mindset because a successful sales conversation starts before you make contact with the ideal prospect. Then, once you start the conversation, you are building rapport and investigating the person's situation.

After that, you're holding the authority/leadership position by explaining the agenda. You're getting a micro-commitment here because they're agreeing to the agenda. Then you're moving into discovering the problem.

You'll stay in this step for a bit because the goal is to uncover their deep problem—the real motivator for wanting to make a change. Then you'll transition into identifying the desired transformation. What is it that they want? What are the new identity, emotional state, and daily life experiences that they desire? *When I get X, I'll feel Y.*

Okay, so that brings us up to speed.

Step 9. Review the Conversation

Now we are at the review stage. This is where you review the conversation you've had so far and get another micro-commitment, meaning you're getting them to agree with you and tell you it's okay to move on by using phrases like this:

HP: "Does this make sense? Yes, cool. Are you okay if I move on? Yes, awesome. Is this resonating with you? Is this helping you gain clarity?"

Micro-commitment questions usually have a simple 'yes' response. You're aiming to have the prospect say 'yes' or to agree with you.

Here's an example of how you'd transition into the review stage…

HP: "Okay, so let's review everything we've covered so far so that I don't miss anything. You told me [describe the problem using their words] and how [use their words to describe their experience that was so hard], which is why you felt motivated to book a call now."

HP: "It makes you feel [describe feeling] that you have to [miss out/not have/feel a certain way]." These are the situations/feelings/experiences that they can't have but want to have because of the problem.

HP: "And you've [state what they've tried to do to fix the problem], but that didn't work because [give reasons]."

HP: "Am I getting everything so far? Yes?" [micro-commitment].

Because the truth is that all your ideal clients really want is [desired outcome]. This is where you paraphrase back to them:

HP: "When you get to [desired goal], you'll feel [desired outcome]."

HP: "Is this correct? Is there anything else important you'd like to add here?"

Then you stop talking. Let them tell you what else is important to them.

Okay, now we're at the part where a lot of practitioners and coaches drop the authority and leadership frame—'the ask'.

Now up to this point you haven't talked at all about your program or service. You did tell them at the beginning that your goal is to identify where they are and what they want; if you have a program or service that will help them get there, you'll share it with them (and otherwise, you'll refer them to the best possible person or program who can help them).

Up to now the call has been all about them because you are truly there for them and, without uncovering details about where they are and where they want to go (the 'diagnosis'), you can't give them any next-step recommendations (the 'prescription').

Let's move to the next step where you'll need to transition to 'the ask', and you'll do this with confidence and certainty. You're still holding the authority and leadership frame.

Step 10. Make the Ask

So we're at the part where you might get sweaty. If I were you, I'd get a couple of black shirts and rotate between them. Even if the person can't see you, you know you have pit stains.

A warning: this is where you might feel inclined to shrink your energetic state. Meaning, this is the part where your body language or tone of voice might change because you feel uncomfortable making 'the ask' because of whatever false beliefs you have about selling.

Your level of certainty and confidence needs to be at 100%. This means that your energy and tone of voice must project confidence and certainty that you have a solution to their problem.

This tip is very important: do not make any decisions for the prospect. You don't get to decide whether or not they can afford the fee or if they're ready to work with you. Your responsibility is to give them your professional recommendations which may or may not be your program based on how the conversation went.

If you don't extend an offer to work with you, two things will happen.

First, you are doing your ideal prospect a massive disservice because you've just led them through a very emotionally charged conversation that has brought them to a place where they're most likely ready to commit. By not confidently making 'the ask', you're leaving them high and dry with no support to move forward.

Secondly, because they are looking for help and you've just led them through this emotionally charged conversation, you've laid the groundwork for them, and they are on the brink of making a commitment. If you don't make 'the ask' with confidence and certainty, they will go find someone else who will. And that person will reap the benefits of all your hard work. It's like you've just set the sale up for someone else to take.

So you're at the place in the conversation where you have to transition to making 'the ask'. Here's an example of how you'd smoothly transition:

HP: "So [name], I am 100% certain that I can help solve this for you because…" or "I'm 100% certain that I can help you go from X to Y because…"

Then you move into sharing a testimonial—you validate their fear by demonstrating capability. If you've gotten results for someone else, then you can get results for them too.

HP: "I'm 100% confident that I can help you because you remind me of [name of client with similar problem], one of my clients. She came to me with [describe the problem]. She started in almost the exact same situation as you." [Describe the situation. Give some reasons (ones that you know will resonate with your ideal prospect because you've already defined your ideal client) why this client was scared to take the next step (those are objections). These reasons could be that she also had no time, her kids play lots of sports, her spouse travels, or she failed so many times before. Describe the emotional pain so that the prospect can relate]."

HP: "But then I helped her by…"

And this is where you describe your program methodology (I will cover this in the next pillar).

HP: "But when I helped her to first do X, then do Y, and when she finally had the right A and got B, she quickly saw C results. It was because she finally had the right system to fix her problem along with the right support." (This is where you describe what the person needs in order to get results.)

You're doing it through sharing a testimonial, so it doesn't feel like a pitch.
And the transition sentence is:

HP: "… and the way that we did that is…"

This is where you describe the phases/steps/sections/modules—you stay high level. You're not using any techno babble or going into detail. Details confuse people. You are going for clarity and certainty.

People want to buy into a system, a process—not modules and PDFs.

The more details you give, the more objections you invite because they will need clarification. All the ideal prospect wants to know is that you have a system—a methodology that will work—and that you're going to make it as easy as possible for them so that they stop feeling (whatever the problem is).

So once you've explained the process and how you're going to help them close the gap from where they are now to where they want to go, you have to make 'the ask'.

Here's an example of how you'd do that:

HP: "If I showed you how to do XYZ so that you could have [desired outcome], are you willing to [describe what steps they need to follow]?"

Stop talking.
Good.

Now the next question is paramount. This is where you get the prospect to tell you how helpful your process or methodology would be.

You say this:

HP: "Good, I'm glad you're willing to do that. Tell me, how do you think having these steps will help you get to [desired goal]?"

Now they have to tell you how your program will help them. They're essentially selling themselves into your program.

Then after they tell you, you ask them the next question:

HP: "What questions do you have for me?"

If you've explained the process well, they likely won't have any questions. You want them to ask you about the price. You want them to ask you about the investment.

If they don't, then you can ask:

HP: "Would you like to discuss the investment?"

You're asking for permission to tell them the price.

HP: "Okay great, the investment is [state the price] and that includes giving you access to [list the program components] so that you can [then sum up how having access to the program will stop the pain and get them to where they want to be]."

The Ask: HP: "Would you like to get started?"

Then stop talking.

Literally do not speak. Hit mute if you need to. Hold the tension for longer than it feels comfortable. Now that you've made 'the ask' and shared the investment, the conversation could go one of two ways.

The first way is that they say 'yes' without objection. If

that's the case, then you move right into processing the payment and enrolling your new ideal client (yay!). This happens sometimes, but more than likely you'll experience the next way.

The second way is that they have questions or objections. Unsurprisingly, this would be where you move into the Handle the Objections step.

Step 11. Handle the Objections

Here's something to think about: objections are just fears disguised. Because you've created your ideal client profile, you should have a list of the major objections that your ideal prospect might have.

And with that being said, this is also where most practitioners and coaches get nervous because they don't want to feel pushy or salesy. But this is the part where you must uphold your authority and leadership mindset the most.

This is where you are drawing a hard line in the sand for your ideal prospect and not letting them take the easy way out. Every time they throw out an objection and you can reassure them that you've got it covered and you relate it back to a process in your methodology, you demonstrate that the issue, whatever it is, is covered—and so it's no longer an issue.

If they throw out the price objection, then you can ask them:

HP: "If I could break apart the full investment price into a monthly payment plan, would that work for you?"

You've just made 'the ask' again.

Then stop talking.

Continue to overcome the objections and continue to ask if they're ready to get started.

Here are some common objections and some language to help you overcome them:

Issue: Not Engaging

HP: "I get the sense that what we've been discussing doesn't feel really important or relevant to you? With [name of your program], we really only work with people who are all in, who are invested, and who are really present and determined to succeed 100%. Can you understand that? Okay… so based on this call so far, I feel like maybe you're not there yet. Is that fair?"

Issue: Needs to Check with Partner First

HP: "I totally understand that you would want to talk about this with your partner first. It's a big decision. Now, I want to be totally forthcoming with you… I have [state number] more calls booked for today, and I only take a certain number of people into [name of your program] at a time in order to ensure that each person receives the best support. What I can do, however, is take a [state dollar amount of deposit] 100% refundable deposit right now to hold your spot."

HP: "If you were to do that, that would secure your spot and save you [state dollar amount of savings] if you decide to pay in full once you chat with your partner. Would you like to take advantage of this option?"

Issue: Financial Objections

HP: "I completely understand that it's a big investment for you. Let's acknowledge that it's scary, and then with your permission, let's dig a bit deeper to find out if it's really about the money or if there's something else holding you back."

HP: "Let me ask you this… if it wasn't for the price, would this be a hell yes for you?"

This answer is important. If they say:
IP: "I'm not sure."
Then you can say:

HP: "[Name], when it comes to these calls/appointments, etc., I really have one goal, and that is to help you figure out if you are a hell yes or a hell no to this program. That's it."

HP: "So what can I clarify for you that's going to get you to a confident *yes* or *no* by the time we finish our conversation? Because the last thing I want to do is leave you feeling confused or indecisive."

This is where they will ask questions, and you can provide further clarification.

If they say:

IP: "I would be a hell yes aside from the price."

Then you can say something like…

HP: "Great. So would it be helpful if we talked about some creative ways that you can find the resources to make this investment?"

HP: "Amazing… would it be helpful for you if I extended the payment plan by two months, bringing the cost down to [state amount per month] for [state number of months]?"

One of the financial objections I've come across is the desire to stay out of debt. So my question to them is:

HP: "If you were to look ahead a year, tell me which option is scarier, being [state number of dollars] in debt or [this is where you would link the reason they booked the call: e.g., you're still 45lb overweight, or you've had to go on medication for diabetes, or whatever the main problem according to them is]?"

Issue: Vomiting Information

HP: "So wait just a second… wait just a second here.

I'm not trying to cut you off, but I do want to make sure that you're getting the most benefit for your time."

HP: "Let's get back to [restate the question here]."

Stop them when they tell you something really juicy.

HP: "Wait a minute… so you're telling me the *real* reason this is important to you is that if you don't [state the problem], you're afraid [your husband is going to leave… etc.]?"

HP: "Hold on a second… did you just say this… first of all, thank you. Thank you for being open and vulnerable. A lot of people get on this call and they just want to stay surface level, and they're not really trying to solve their actual problem, and I can tell this isn't you."

Issue: Person on the Call Is Overconfident

HP: "Why did you book this call? If you already have a solution, can you tell me what you're hoping to get out of this call if you feel like you already have this handled?"

HP: "What do you feel like you're missing that made you book this call?"

HP: "Let me say this: there are two kinds of people who come on this call. There's the type of person who has failed a lot, is struggling, and just really wants to finally feel better. To be honest, that's most of the people that come to me."

HP: "The second type of person is the person who is already feeling better but is looking for [whatever your person is looking for]. This is the type of person who has experienced some success and thinks that to get deeper results they just need to be told what to do, which in my professional experience isn't the case. Actually, it's the opposite. When you go deeper, there's more stuff that comes up that needs to be supported. Does that make sense?"

HP: "Okay, great, then do you feel that investing in [state name of your program] would be your next best move if your goal is to [desired outcome]?"

Once you've got their commitment, you continue with enrollment.

Step 12. Proceed with Enrollment

This step is the most exciting because this is where the ideal prospect becomes an ideal client and you get paid!

We've found that regardless of whether the ideal prospect is sitting in front of you, or if you're on the phone or Skype or

Zoom, it's critical to take payment on the call. If you end the conversation without taking payment, it's likely that the ideal client will regret their decision, fear will take over, and they'll back out.

Without getting too technical here, you want to have a way to take a virtual payment. This could mean sending a PayPal invoice while the person is still on the phone with you so you can make sure they accept it and pay it, or you could set up a checkout page where you enter the person's payment details. The second way is my preferred method.

Regardless, you want to do your best to get their payment completed while they are still on the call with you. Then once their payment is completed, you can give your new ideal client their next steps.

Well that was fun, wasn't it? We have two more pillars left to cover, and then you're off to the races.

Action Steps

- Use the 12 Steps to Getting the YES! Framework to create your own sales script.
- Get ten volunteers to practice making "the ask" with you.
- Record your sales conversations so you can critique them afterwards.

Chapter 9

Pillar 4:
BUILD THE METHODOLOGY (THE SIGNATURE PROGRAM)

I'll never forget the day I got my first update from the nutritionist I hired to run the WOW! Weight Loss program. I had just brought her onboard because I was about to have a baby and about to go on maternity leave. It's worth mentioning here that when you work for yourself in whatever capacity, maternity leave isn't really a thing. But I knew that I would need to take at least three months off work, and at that point I had my program running in multiple locations. I didn't want to have to shut my business down, so I had to figure out a way to keep it running while I did the mom thing.

The months were flying by, and my boss, Tara asked me what I was planning on doing with the program while I was off. I was about six months pregnant at that point, and she was asking because she wanted to know if I was going to offer one last program before I gave birth. I knew she was thinking about the sales goals, even though she didn't mention it. Up to that point I hadn't really given any thought to what I was going to do. I was too consumed with keeping up with the clients and the business, given that I was dead tired and had total 'pregnancy brain'. If you've ever been pregnant, then you know what I'm talking about. It's like your brain completely stops working and turns to mush.

Hmm… what was I going to do with the program while I was off on fake maternity leave?

This was one of those times when the books I had studied for business advice weren't helpful. There was no book about what to do with your business while the business owner goes off to have a baby (or gets sick for an extended period of time or has surgery or wants to go on a long vacation). Oh wait… there is now! But I digress. There was no framework for me to follow so I did what I always do: I made it up.

Not only did my time at Weight Watchers help me to build out the WOW! Weight Loss program, it gave me a business model that I could copy. The owner of Weight Watchers wasn't the one running the program. There were coaches and support staff running the entire operation. So now I had my answer… I was going to hire a nutritionist to run the program for me so that I could take time off. So that's what I told my boss. I told her that I was going to hire another nutritionist to take my place for a while so that the program could continue to run without me.

I remember the look on her face when I told her my plan. "Are you sure that's a good idea? What if she screws it all up? What if the clients dislike her? What if she fails to get them the same kind of results you do? What if she is so good that the clients want to stay with her when you get back?"

Jeez... those are a lot of 'what ifs'! "Well," I said, "my choices are to shut the program down and not help any clients or make any money for however long; or I can go with plan B and hire someone and take my chances."

So that's what I did. I hired a nutritionist to take over for me. I was only able to do that because the WOW! Weight Loss program ran like a machine. By this point it was so systematized that all I had to do was to teach this new person my system and hope that she didn't screw it all up.

I don't even know how I did it since my brain was mush, but before I went into labor, I had found a nutritionist to take over the program, trained her, and helped her to fill her first program. I was able to shadow her and mentor her so that she ran the program exactly how I wanted her to. This wasn't a case of saying "here's all my clients—make it your own." I was very clear that she was running my program and working for me. Although I am not a huge fan of the Weight Watchers program, I am eternally grateful that it exists because it saved my ass more times than I can count.

It turns out that hiring that nutritionist was one of the best moves I made because it opened the door to expanding the program into more locations. Now that there were two of us, this meant that I was able to help more clients and make more money.

The lesson I learned from that experience was that *it didn't need to be me*. Up to that point in my career, I was operating under the very false assumption that I needed to be the one to directly work with the clients—that I was the only one who was capable of teaching them, supporting them, and answering their questions. Nope. Not true. The WOW! Weight Loss program did the work, and the nutritionist was there to work the program.

Ego in check!

In all fairness to me and to you, the reason that I thought that it had to be me was because that is the way I was taught. I wasn't shown that there was another more leveraged and profitable way to grow my business and that it could be very successful, even if I wasn't the one directly working with clients. Once I realized this, it was like a whole new world opened up to me, and I could see the potential of WOW! Weight Loss.

What I'm about to dive into in Pillar 4: Build the Methodology (The Signature Program) is a paradigm shift away from how you were taught. I get that. But it doesn't mean that it won't work. All it means is that there is another way for you to grow your business that you are unaware of right now. Trust me, having a results-based methodology as the framework of your signature program is a game-changer. Having a signature program that you use as the main program offer in your business is how you will grow your business beyond any measure of success you previously thought possible.

Now before you revert into, "But Lori, I'm a [insert your professional designation] and I don't know how I would do that," I want you to read through this entire chapter. All I'm asking is that you keep an open mind and instead of thinking, "I don't know how this would work," reframe the thought to, "How can I make this work?" I've taught this pillar of the

Health Expert Business Model to over two thousand practitioners and coaches from all over the world, even to some whose first language isn't English. We have thousands of our clients using signature programs in their businesses, and so if it works for them, I promise it will work for you too. All it requires from you is a willingness to see that there is another way, aside from directly working 1:1 and custom-creating programs for each person, to get your ideal clients the promised outcomes they desire.

Pillar 4: Build the Methodology (The Signature Program) is the foundation that your entire business is built upon. Without having a signature program, you do not have a scalable way to grow your business, get clients, and ditch your day job. You'll be stuck trading hours for dollars, you'll be overrun with manual busy-work, and you'll cap your earning potential because there are only so many time slots available in the day for you to work directly with those clients. Once those time slots are full, you can't take on anyone else. Plus, and maybe you've experienced this already… it's exhausting to work 1:1 with clients all day. You end up feeling like a robot repeating yourself over and over because 99.9% of your clients all have the same problem, challenges, and questions.

If I hadn't created WOW! Weight Loss and became an expert at creating signature programs, I would not have the level of success I have right now; I am certain of that. As I mentioned earlier, this is the book I would have paid any amount of money to have when I was first starting to grow my business. If you get nothing else from this book (which I hope doesn't happen!) I want you to get this:

Having a signature program is the foundation your business is built upon and gives you the ability to grow your business beyond any measure of success you ever thought possible.

So let's not waste another minute, okay?

What Is a Results-Based Method?

Why did an ideal prospect subscribe to your value-based lead magnet? Why are they in your world? It's because they have a problem that you seem to be able to help them get rid of.

But how?

How are you going to get rid of the problem your ideal clients have in a repeatable and scalable way?

Mashing together a bunch of habits, providing 37 different to-dos, and giving meal plans and pages of theory won't cut it. You are no longer creating individualized protocols or programs for each client that you see. That's the old school way of operating, and we've already discussed that we're done with that model. Don't worry, I've got a way for you to work 1:1 with clients that is coming up in Pillar 5, but before you dive deep with clients and personalize their programs, they need to implement the fundamentals that support deeper healing.

Agree?

Method: *a particular form of procedure for accomplishing or approaching something, especially a systematic or established one.*

How are you going to get rid of the problem your ideal clients have in a repeatable and scalable way? You are going to develop, based on your own experience, professional education, and health/well-being/coaching philosophy, a step-by-step method that delivers on the promise to alleviate the pain and provide the transformation.

Say what?

Yes, you will have your very own method for getting results for your ideal clients, and your method is the thing that you're going to become known for. Remember, you promised to keep an open mind. This is where I need you to fulfill that promise. It's okay if you don't know the 'how' yet. I'm going to teach it to you. All I need is for you to ask yourself, "How can I make this work?"

Have you ever put together a piece of furniture?

When you put together furniture or anything like that, there's an instruction manual that gives you the step-by-step instructions, including descriptions for each part and which parts you need, starting from Step 1. The instructions tell you which part to use, and if they're good instructions, they will walk you through how to use the part. Then you move on to Step 2, which builds on Step 1. If you don't do Step 1 correctly, Step 2 won't work. You follow the instructions step-by-step until your chair is built. And if you skip steps or miss a part, it's possible that the chair will break when someone sits in it.

Now think about the person writing the instructions for the chair. They had to start with a finished chair and work backward. They had to know what the finished chair would look like before they could instruct anyone to put it together. They had to know each part, the order in which the parts needed to be used, and how to explain how to use the parts so that the person reading the instructions could follow them.

Because if the instructions suck and the majority of the people who buy the chair can't follow them, then the company will have a customer service problem resulting in many requests for refunds. Even if the fully assembled chair is the best chair on the face of the planet, if the majority of the people who buy the chair can't follow the instructions and figure out how to build the chair … well, then the quality of the chair is irrelevant.

It's not like everyone who buys the chair can call up the maker of the chair to ask specific questions. "What if I don't have a screwdriver? What do I do instead?" The maker of the chair and the writer of the instructions have to consider their customers and make it as simple and easy as possible to build the chair.

So you're going to think about the end result that your ideal clients want—what is the pain that they want alleviated? Then you're going to put together step-by-step instructions that they can easily follow so that by the time they're done working with you, they get the desired result—no more pain—that then gives them the opportunity to have all the feelings and experiences they desire to have because they're not suffering anymore.

"Okay Lori, I get that I need to create a step-by-step program that my ideal clients can follow, but what's the difference between a method and a signature program?"

You are totally on the ball, my friend. I'm going to explain it now and then walk you through how to create your method and your signature program.

What Is a Signature Program?

I'm not a fan of wearing makeup. But I like how I look when I fill in my brows, so I went to Sephora, which is a high-end makeup store in Canada, and asked the very beautiful sales associate (who had perfect makeup) for some help with finding the right brow utensil. She looked at me and said, "You can't just do your brows. You need a complete face."

I was kinda shocked. "Um... a complete face? I'm pretty sure my face is complete but okay, tell me more."

I ended up spending hundreds of dollars on makeup that day because she took the time to explain what it meant to have a 'complete face'—that doing my brows was just one part of 'completing the face'—and then went on to show me all the different makeup products I would need, the order to use them in, and how to use them to get a 'complete face', which was 'the look' I was going for.

Think of the results-based method you're going to create as one component of your signature program. It's the brows... but you need a 'complete face' in order to achieve your desired look.

A signature program combines the different required elements to truly deliver the promised outcome—no more pain. Having a results-based method in and of itself won't cut it. Sure, the results-based method is a critical part, but we know that having the steps to follow doesn't mean that your ideal clients will walk along them.

Think about the other elements that your ideal clients need in order to deliver the promised result—no more pain.

The Signature Program includes the following elements:

- Results-Based Methodology
- Accountability
- Coaching
- Community

When you combine these elements together, you have a 'complete face'.

The Role the Signature Program Plays in Your Business:

From 2008 to 2014, I only offered one program in my nutrition practice, the WOW! Weight Loss program. That was it. I had a method that worked to get my clients results, and so I used that method and the additional support elements (accountability, support, and, if applicable, community) to work with clients in a variety of ways.

I'm lazy. I like doing the work one time and then leveraging it for as long as possible in as many ways as possible. I spent over a year creating the WOW! Weight Loss program, and I wasn't about to let all that hard work go to waste. The WOW! Weight Loss program got results for clients, so why would I use anything else? Why would I spend time creating an entirely different method when the one I had worked? I became known as the WOW! Girl, and people expected me to use that method to help them get their desired results—weight loss.

Except there were clients who didn't want to be a part of the group. There were times in the year when it didn't make sense to run the full 12-week program or when I knew that having a short challenge would be a better sales offer. So I took the path of least resistance and modified the method and the additional support to suit the situation.

I used the WOW! Weight Loss program in a variety of situations:

- My original 12-week group
- Four-, six-, and eight-week groups
- A 1:1 program at a higher price for those people who didn't want to do the group
- A two-day workshop version of the program
- Corporate wellness programs via Skype

Did a lightbulb just come on? I hope so. When you know your ideal client and you're clear on the problem they want to get rid of, you're able to create a signature program that delivers that outcome and then use that signature program as the cornerstone of your business. You are able to consistently enroll clients into your signature program because the program is finished, set up, and automated.

Wanna know how to create a signature program, set it up, and automate it? Good, because I'm about to tell you ... so let's keep going.

As I've mentioned, I've been teaching practitioners and coaches how to create signature programs since 2014. I've taught registered dietitians, sexologists, physiotherapists, reiki masters, massage therapists, licensed therapists, medical doctors, nurses, cancer coaches, naturopathic doctors, nutritionists, health coaches, aromatherapists, meditation teachers, yoga instructors, culinary nutrition experts... seriously, you name an alternative health professional, and I'm sure we've had them as a client.

There has never been a single idea that any of our 2,000+ clients have brought to the table that couldn't be turned into a results-based method and packaged as a signature program. Not once. Even if you are someone who sells a physical product or needs to lay hands on your patients or clients, you can create a signature program that provides additional support that is needed in order to get your ideal clients the results they desire.

Signature Program Creation Process

Here are the eight steps for creating your signature program:

1. Validate the Idea & Solidify the Outcome.
2. Create the Method.
3. Record the Content.
4. Add Additional Support.
5. Implement Program Delivery.
6. Confirm Program Specifics.
7. Collect Feedback and Iterate.
8. Put It All Together.

Yes, I'm going to go through each part of the signature program creation process, but before I do that, let me assure you that you can create your method and signature program in six to eight weeks. We have clients, some of whom work full time with kids at home, who follow this creation process and get their entire signature program created and ready to beta test within this timeframe. It shouldn't take you six months to create your method, collect feedback, and package it together as your signature program.

So let me get started!

Step 1. Validate the Idea & Solidify the Outcome.

In this first step, we're going to do the crucial work of validating your signature program idea and solidifying the results-based outcome that your program delivers. This is where you determine the outcome that your ideal client wants so you can put together the method that delivers that outcome.

Before I go any further, I need to clear up something extremely important, so please pay attention. There is a difference between the outcome that the ideal client wants and the method you'll use to get them the result. Here's an example of what I mean:

Let's say your ideal client is a burnt-out, stressed-out mom who doesn't take any time for herself. She is always tired, anxious, and emotional. She's not sleeping well, and she can't seem to get herself on track. She wants to have energy to be a good mom, she wants to feel present, and she wants to be able to show up in a way of which she's proud. She's tried yoga, meditation, detox, and therapy, and she is still tired, impatient, and annoyed. That's how she would describe her situation.

The problem is that she's tired, irritable, and anxious.

The outcome she wants is to be a calm, energetic, and good mom.

As the practitioner or coach, it's your job to create a signature program that gets her from problem to outcome. The way you're going to do this is to decide on a 'course of treatment'—your method—that will fix the real problem. Because the symptoms she's experiencing aren't the real problem, they are symptoms being caused by the underlying real problem—the root.

By utilizing your personal experience, professional education, philosophy, and scope of practice, you get to 'diagnose' the real problem. The method is what you'll create to fix the 'root-cause' problem, which will then stop the symptoms as she experiences them so that she can achieve her desired outcome.

Let's go back to our hypothetical ideal client. You may decide that the 'root cause' is her stress hormones. Or you may decide that it's her thyroid. Or you may decide that it's her blood sugar. As the practitioner or coach, you decide, according to your experience and expertise, the 'root-cause' of the problem.

Will the program you create stop your ideal client's pain so that by the time they're done working with you, they'll get the outcome they want?

How to Validate Your Program Idea & Solidify the Outcome

Write down the idea you have for your program (e.g., thyroid, mindset, stress, acne, weight loss).

Go back to your ideal client profile and review the following:

- The symptoms that they complain about the most
- The problem according to the client
- Their hopes and dreams
- Why they want to get rid of the problem
- What they've tried to get rid of the problem

Now go back to your idea. Don't worry about what content to put into the method yet. Does your idea or area of expertise solve the problem according to your ideal client and deliver their hopes and dreams? Can you see how creating X method (your idea) solves the problem according to your ideal client?

For example, let's go back to the burnt-out mom. If your idea was to create a thyroid program but you defined your ideal client as the mom I described above, would creating a thyroid program work for that mom? Maybe...

Or does it only work for the mom *if* you know she has a thyroid problem? If it only works *if* the mom has a thyroid problem, then basing your entire method and signature program around a thyroid program isn't the best idea if you want to work with all moms who feel as I've described above—or you can adjust your ideal client profile to be specific to a mom who has a diagnosed thyroid condition and feels the way I described above. Then you've become an expert in working with moms who are tired, burnt-out, irritable, etc. because they have a thyroid issue, and it just so happens that you have a thyroid program that can help them to feel better.

Here's another common example that I often see with practitioners and coaches. Your idea is to create a leaky gut/digestive healing program. You have expertise in this area and really want to focus your business on digestive health. Cool. Except when you do your ideal client profile, the biggest problem your ideal client is dealing with is weight loss. But you don't want to offer a weight loss program. You want to offer a digestive healing program.

You can totally create a digestive healing program, but when it comes time to sell it, you've got to sell them what they want and give them what they need. What they want is to lose weight. The reason they can't is because their digestive system is messed up. So you've got to communicate to them via your content that the reason nothing has worked before is because of their digestive system, and until they fix their gut, they won't be able to lose weight, which is what they really want. So you're *not* running a weight loss program, but you are solving the problem as they experience it—they can't lose weight. Because I'll tell you, if you tried to sell that ideal client a gut healing program without tying together gut healing equals weight loss, they wouldn't buy it because all they care about is losing weight.

Think about what your ideal client wants. Why are they coming to you?

Will the idea for your program deliver the outcome that the ideal client wants?

Yes, awesome! So now that you've validated your idea, let's move into the fun part: creating the outline for your method.

Step 2. Create the Method.

Picture this scene: I'm sitting on the floor of Chapters bookstore with every single fat loss and hormone balancing book they had at the time spread out all around me, opened to the table of contents pages, along with an array of colored pens and two notebooks. I had no intention of buying any of those books. I was doing research. Why didn't I go to a library? Because the library doesn't have Starbucks. #priorities

When I told you that Weight Watchers and books saved my career, I wasn't exaggerating. I used those books to figure out how to create the outline for the WOW! Weight Loss program. Yes, Weight Watchers was good, but I wanted to teach my ladies more than what they included in their program. I wanted my ladies to understand what was going on inside their bodies, why they felt the way they did, and how their digestive system and hormones were intertwined with their weight. I wanted them to know about macros, calories, nutrient density, the fullness factor, food labels, health washing, gluten, proper digestion, sleep, stress, goal setting, meal planning, and literally every other thing I was ever taught.

My first program outline was seven pages long! I'm not kidding. And those pages only included topics, no other details. I felt like I needed to download every single thing I knew about food, nutrition, and weight loss into their already overwhelmed, confused, and tired brains. I felt like unless I taught them everything that I knew that they wouldn't feel like they were getting their money's worth.

I couldn't have been more wrong.

Sitting on the floor, night after night, taking notes from those fat loss, diet, and hormone balancing books, I realized something critical: the only information that any of those books included was specific to the reader getting the desired result. The chapters were specific, and I could draw a line from the chapter content directly to the outcome. No fluff. No extra, nice-to-know stuff. For example, none of the fat loss books (at that time circa 2009) talked about eating organic—whether the chicken breast or apple was organic or not didn't really have any bearing on getting the reader to lose weight. The other thing those books didn't include was long scientific explanations about why the recommendations were being given. Most of them didn't even have references. Oh, the horror!

Having reviewed over 30 books, I noticed a pattern that helped me reduce the number of topics to 12. Each chapter was focused on one concept. Each one contained a short lesson with actionable strategies for the reader to do that included support materials to help with implementation. And the steps those books recommended seemed so simple, almost too simple. But given that I had no idea what I was doing, I decided *not* to reinvent the wheel and just follow the example that *all* those books had in common.

I'm going to outline the five parts necessary to create the

method. I don't want you to end up with a seven-page outline that turns into a textbook instead of a results-based program.

There are five parts to creating the method:

Part # 1: Define the Outcome Your Program Promises.
Part # 2: Define the Root Cause and Determine Your Philosophy.
Part # 3: Create the Outline.
Part # 4: Refine the Outcome.
Part # 5: Create the Content.

Part # 1: Define the Outcome Your Program Promises.

The good news is that you've already solidified the outcome that your ideal client wants. What is the problem your method solves? What is the desire that it fulfills? You got this.

In order to create your outline, you need to be very clear on one specific outcome the method promises. For example, weight loss, increased energy, better sleep, and better focus are not one specific outcome. Sure, the method you create might deliver all these outcomes, but pick one to create the method for. Your clients will also get the sprinkles as an added bonus.

Part # 2: Define the Root Cause and Determine Your Philosophy.

The outcome and root cause are not the same thing. The outcome is no more fatigue, more energy, and the ability to show up as a calm, present, and loving mom. The root cause is blood sugar (or whatever you determine it to be).

The root cause is the big thing causing the symptoms, which is what the ideal client perceives the problem to be. What is the cause of the symptoms? This is where you turn to your professional education, science, research, and philosophy. In order for you to create a method to stop the pain and deliver the desired outcome, you need to know what the root cause is.

When I was creating WOW! Weight Loss, I decided, based on my own experience, research, and philosophy, that the root cause of my ideal client's inability to lose weight and stick to a diet was blood sugar. I pinned the problem they experienced on blood sugar and insulin. So then I created a program that taught them how to eat in a way that would keep their blood sugar stable, even if they drank wine, ate popcorn, or ate chocolate.

Let's say you want to focus on getting rid of acne. The problem, as the ideal client experiences it, is ugly, embarrassing, and painful acne. No matter what they try, nothing works.

Based on your expertise and scope of practice, you might decide that the reason they have acne is because they have gut issues. Or you might decide that the reason they have acne is because of overexposure to toxins.

It doesn't actually matter what you decide so long as you decide something. The point is, you must define a root cause so that you can decide the course of treatment to address it. I know, of course, that there might be more than one root cause.

Here's an example. Let's say that you want to work with ideal clients who are totally stressed out. Your area of expertise is meditation, and you want to create a meditation program to help your ideal clients reduce stress. That's cool, good idea.

But what is causing the stress? Lifestyle factors and cortisol. Just teaching them to meditate will most likely not reduce the level of stress they feel because you're not addressing any of the other factors. Because you know the root cause—lifestyle factors (cortisol)—you can add elements into your method to teach them meditation and address lifestyle factors, ensuring that they get the desired result.

Think about your philosophy, expertise, and scope of practice. Given the symptoms that your ideal client experiences and the problem they want solved, what, according to you, is the root cause of those symptoms? And if you address the root cause, will the ideal client get the desired outcome?

Part # 3: Create the Outline.

Here comes the fun part, brainstorming. Now you've identified the outcome the program delivers and the root cause, it's time to create your method outline.

The method is the steps and actions that your ideal clients need to follow in order to get the desired result. Putting together many habits or random actions doesn't usually lead to a desired result. Keeping in mind your area of expertise and scope of practice; what information does your ideal client need to learn? And more importantly, what actions do they need to take (and in what order) to get the desired outcome?

The program outline is made up of four parts:

1. **Phases/Steps:** Having phases or steps isn't mandatory, but they are helpful when it comes to organizing and talking about your program. For example: the XXX program has X phases. Each phase has Y number of modules. Each module has Z number of learning lessons with corresponding action tasks.

2. **Modules:** These are the big overarching categories that make up the structure of your method.

3. **Learning Lessons:** These are the lessons that go under each module. What are you going to teach, and why does it matter? What do your clients need to learn so that when the time comes to do the action, everything makes sense?

4. **Action Tasks:** These are the specific actions that are connected to the learning lessons. Not every single learning lesson has an action task, but there should be specific action tasks that your ideal client should have to complete.

Here's What You Do Next:

Sticky notes: Get a permanent marker and three packs of sticky notes (size doesn't matter), each in a different color. One color is for the modules, one is for learning lessons, and one is for action tasks. You will organize into phases when you're done with your outline.

Find a wall: Find an open space somewhere in your home where you can spread your sticky notes all over the wall.

Brainstorm: Start by writing the outcome and root cause (e.g., get rid of fatigue/blood sugar) on a sticky note, and put it on the center of the wall.

Based on the outcome and root cause, I find it helpful to start by brainstorming 8-12 overarching modules. These are key categories that will make up the big steps of your method.

Then for each module, brainstorm the learning lessons and action tasks you *could* include. You're going to end up with a big brain dump of modules, learning lessons, and action tasks. That's okay. You're going to drill down and refine your outline.

Once you've brain-dumped everything you can think of, you should organize your modules, lessons, and action tasks. This is where it's helpful to think of your method as phases.

Phases => Modules => Learning Lessons => Action Tasks

As you organize, remove any fluff or nice-to-have information. If the idea on the sticky note is not directly tied to your ideal client getting the outcome (i.e., if you removed it, would they still get the outcome), remove it. There's only one caveat: keep the idea if you feel strongly that it is a critical factor to *how* they get the desired result. This is where you use your judgment and expertise to decide what content to remove and what to keep.

Ask yourself the following questions to help you prune your outline:

- What are the big two-to-four phases that my ideal client needs to go through?

- Which modules correspond to each phase?
- Are the modules in the correct order?
- Are the learning lessons in the correct order?
- Are the action tasks in the correct order, and do they connect with the learning lessons in the modules?
- Do the learning lessons teach information that is 'need to know' or 'nice to know'?
- Could you follow the action tasks at a 90% compliance rate? (Because if *you* can't at 90%, then your ideal client likely won't even hit a 50% compliance rate.)
- Are there any modules, learning lessons, or action tasks that don't fit or that aren't necessary in order for your ideal client to get their desired result?
- If you took away the learning lessons and just left the action tasks, would the ideal client get the desired outcome?

Now is the time to refine your outline so that it is as results-based as possible.

Part # 4: Refine the Outcome.

At this point you should have a fairly concise outline that consists of your phases, modules, learning lessons, and action tasks. Now that you have drilled down and removed all the fluff and nice-to-have content, it's time to ensure that what you have in your outline is what *should* be there.

Important: Keep in mind that whatever you end up with now is the first iteration of your method (and signature program), and I guarantee that you will modify, if not redo, the entire method after you put 10 or more clients through the program. *The goal is to take imperfect action and to get the first iteration finished.*

Now check that the modules, including the learning lessons and action tasks, are outcome-based.

Ask: how are this module, these learning lessons, and these action tasks going to solve the problem for the ideal client and deliver the promised outcome?

Write down the outcome for each module. After the ideal client finishes Y module, they should know ABC and do XYZ, which is directly related to solving the problem because [fill in the blank].

You should be able to communicate how each module is connected to solving the problem. I don't want you to guess here. If you're not sure why you've included a module, learning lesson, or action task, other than you *think* you need to, that's going to impede your confidence when it comes time to sell the program. This is where spending time referring to other programs or conducting research is crucial so that you have evidence for why you've included the modules, learning lessons, and action tasks.

Once you're done refining your outline, give it to a colleague to review. Let them poke holes in it. Don't tell them who your ideal client is or the problem your method solves. Give them the outline and ask them to tell you what problem you're solving.

When I do an outline review for a client, I don't want to know many details before I review it. I want fresh eyes to see if I can determine what the problem they're solving is and what the outcome would be. If I can't make out a specific problem and outcome, then that signals to my client that they need to be more specific with their modules, learning lessons, and action tasks.

Yes, this is time consuming. But this is the method that is the cornerstone of your signature program, which is the foundation of your business. It's okay to take time, but don't waste too much striving for perfection on the first go; six to eight weeks is all you need.

Resistance: This is where most practitioners and coaches start to second-guess themselves and to overthink their method. This happens either because you're unsure what you've created will get results for clients, or because you're unsure if what you have is enough to warrant the fee you want to charge. Maybe you're having second thoughts that anyone will even buy your program. Although these fears are a normal part of the creative process, they still are annoying. Don't let them interfere with finishing your method.

My suggestion is to give yourself a deadline to finish the method outline and find an accountability partner. In my experience, nothing works better than being held accountable to someone you really do not want to disappoint.

Part # 5: Create the Content.

You're almost there. Give yourself a pat on the back!

At this point you should have a finished outline detailing the modules, learning lessons, and action tasks that fall under each. Notice I didn't tell you how many learning lessons or action tasks to include. I've withheld those guidelines for a very specific reason. You are the expert in your field, not me. I'm giving you the framework to follow, but I don't know what's best for your method and your ideal client. You do. Trust your own judgment and know that this is the first iteration. The goal is to finish it so that you can collect feedback.

You are going to use your outline to develop the learning lessons and action tasks. This is where you script the learning lessons and design the action tasks for your ideal clients to follow. It is the part that takes the longest because you are creating the entire method from scratch.

Tips for Teaching Online:

- Create the content for the beginner and the person with the least amount of knowledge. Everyone will be able to follow along.
- Set expectations from the start by having an overview video that explains how the program is laid out and the next steps.
- Create your learning lessons like you're teaching a class—opening, summary of what they'll learn, teaching points, and conclusion.
- Include a review of the previous learning lesson to connect the learning lessons to each other.
- Respect your ideal clients' time and ability to consume the content by keeping content concise and digestible.
- Add in your personality, stories, and examples to

make the content fun, engaging, relatable, and easy to consume.

Tips for Creating Learning Lessons:

* Each learning lesson should start and end in the same way. For example, "Welcome back. In this lesson I'm going to cover XYZ." Then at the conclusion, "We're at the end of this lesson, where you learned XYZ. Now it's time to take action, so move to the action task now. I'll see you in the next lesson."
* It's okay to have multiple learning lessons in each module, but aim to keep each learning lesson under 15 minutes in length.
* Each learning lesson should cover a singular topic.
* All you need is a script. You don't need PowerPoints (you'll be audio recording the learning lessons until you need to do a physical demonstration, which would be a video).
* You should figure out the path of least resistance for yourself. If you can teach a lesson from an outline, go for it. I personally need to script each lesson word for word. It takes longer but it gives me more confidence.
* After you've scripted each lesson, read it out loud to make sure it's clear and it flows.
* If you are explaining a concept that you want your ideal client to take action on, then make sure you have an action task associated with the concept.

Tips for Creating Action Tasks:

- Action tasks are instructions, so give sequential steps to take to complete the action. Include all relevant information. For example, if you want your clients to include a protein with their meals, then give them a list of the proteins to include, the portion size, and any other relevant information they need to add a protein to their meal.
- The ideal client should be able to follow the instructions to complete the action task without needing any other input from you.
- The action tasks should be followable with or without the learning lesson.
- You should create checklists, step-by-step instructions, plans, guides, audio, or video to walk the ideal client through following the action task.
- The instructions should be as simple to follow as possible.
- The action tasks should be given to a colleague to see if they can follow the tasks without asking you for further details.

Okay, now you've created your program outline, the method, and the program content. Good job! Let's move onto the next step … recording your method content.

Step 3. Record the Content

Funny story... the first version of The Wellness Business Academy (WBA) was a 12-month program. I had mapped out the content—all the modules, learning lessons, and action tasks. I had every intention of spending a couple of weeks to record all the content at once so it would be done, and then I could just show up and coach. I didn't want to scramble to record the content and then worry about uploading it before the module was released.

Well, that most certainly did not happen. This was 2014 and I was still running my nutrition practice full time, my daughter was six, my son was three, and my online business was growing quickly. There were no extra hours in my already 16- to 18-hour workday. So, I took imperfect action and recorded the modules at 4:00 a.m. the day they were to be released. Bryan, my then-husband, who was handling all the tech at the time, would load them into our membership site, and the email would be scheduled to go out at noon EDT. To be totally honest, there were a couple of times during the creation of that first WBA iteration where I was late with the content. One of the kids didn't sleep and waking up at 4:00 a.m. to record was not happening that day, so I had to push back the release of the upcoming module. Oops.

Even though I wanted to do a face-to-camera video with slides and make it all fancy, that was impossible given the time constraints. Instead, I took the path of least resistance so I could just get it done. I created worksheets in Word and converted them into PDFs, and I recorded audio lessons to go along with them. No PowerPoints. No transcripts. No fancy-designed PDFs. I just needed to get the content recorded. And I did. Too bad I changed it all about six months later—and four more times after that!

Now that you have your method solidified, your fluff stripped, and your content outlined, scripted, and ready to go, it's time to record your content. Remember: *take the path of least resistance, and don't make your content fancy.* I guarantee that you will iterate this first version of your method at least three times before you're happy with it, so do yourself a favor and don't waste time, energy, or financial resources trying to make your method content fancy.

Based on many years of creating signature programs and working with thousands of practitioners and coaches, I know that there are many ways to get your method content recorded. In this section, I'm going to walk you through the fastest, least expensive way to record your content and create your worksheets.

Choosing the Recording Type

There are two ways to record your content: audio and video.

There is one way to create your handouts and worksheets: Use Google doc or Word docs and save them as PDFs.

For content, audio should be your default. The only reason you should use video is if you have to physically demonstrate something so that your ideal client can follow along with the demonstration. Some examples would be if you're demonstrating physical movement exercises or walking someone through a recipe. Otherwise, for this first iteration, I want you to script your learning lessons and audio record them; do the same for the action tasks if you feel verbal instruction is needed.

Do not waste your time creating PowerPoints to voice record them as video. To create the action task worksheets or any other paper-type handouts you want to provide, simply use Google docs or Microsoft Word and save them as PDFs. Do not waste your time trying to design your handouts or worksheets using online programs like Canva or spend money on a graphic designer. At this stage, none of that is necessary.

The only time I suggest including face-to-camera video is to record a welcome video and a finale video that your ideal clients will watch at the beginning and end of your signature program. This isn't at all mandatory, but it's a nice added touch.

Here's a list of equipment and software you need to record, edit, and create your worksheets:

- Computer
- Audio recording platform like Zoom (it's free and you can use it to record both audio-only and face-to-camera video)
- Screenflow for editing
- Microsoft Word or Google docs
- Adobe PDF
- Optional: if you want to improve the sound quality, you can purchase an external microphone (Shure or Yeti are good brands priced under $100 and available on Amazon)

Terms & Platforms

Since I know tech issues can provoke anxiety, I'm going to introduce some terminology and some platform recommendations that are important for you to know. These will pop up again when it is time to organize how you're going to deliver your program. None of these are requirements, but they are recommendations.

Term: Hosting/hosted

This refers to cloud storage where you upload your content and it's hosted in a cloud-based platform. You will need to host your content in a cloud-based platform and provide download links to your ideal clients so they can access the program content.

Hosting Platform: Amazon S3

Term: Download link

This is the URL link that the cloud-based platform will give you for each piece of content that you host. You will take the links and use them in your program delivery emails.

Term: MP3

This is the file type you will save audio files as.

Term: MP4

This is the file type you will save video files as.

Term: Hyperlink

This is where you link words (e.g., 'click here to download') to the download link that the cloud-based platform gave you for each piece of content that you hosted. The ideal client will click the hyperlinked words, and the content will automatically start to download.

Platform: YouTube

This is a free platform that we suggest you host your videos on (if applicable).

Platform: Amazon S3

This is a platform that we suggest you host your audio and PDFs on.

Content Organization

It's important that you keep your content files organized so that you can easily access them when needed. If you're anything like me, you'll create a document or an audio file, name it something random, and then not be able to find it again. Let's not do that, okay?

Tips for Organizing Your Content on Your Desktop:

- Create a dedicated folder on your desktop and name it 'Signature Program' (everything you create for your signature program will be saved inside this folder).
- Create subfolders for each of your modules and label them 1.NAME | 2.NAME, etc.
- Save the program content that you create in the

- module subfolders using this naming convention: 'Lesson Y Name of Learning Lesson', 'Action Task Z Name of Action Task'.
- Avoid saving individual pieces of content (audio, video, Word docs, and PDFs) to your desktop instead of putting them in the correct folders.

Tips for Recording

- Script all content first and then record.
- Pause after you make a mistake and then continue. Don't start recording again from the beginning—you can edit it later.
- Put out 10 times your normal energy and talk with a smile so you come across as livelier and more engaging.
- Pace yourself and take breaks.
- Plan your time and schedule an extra 20 minutes longer than needed to record each learning lesson and to create each handout.

Holy crap! You have your own expert method, the content is created, and now it's recorded. I hope you feel like a superhero.

"Lori, I have a question."

"Hit me..."

"How do I include 1:1 calls?"

Ooooh. Good one. Let's talk about adding in additional support strategies to round out your signature program.

Step 4. Add Additional Support

Every now and again, I get emails from practitioners and coaches that ask, "Do you ever take on any 1:1 clients?" At this point, I'd rather give someone 30 minutes of my time for free than take on a private client. I believe in the power of community so strongly that I don't believe it's in anyone's best interest to work with a practitioner or coach solely in a 1:1 capacity.

That said, there are some instances where 1:1 work is a must:

* Licensed practitioners have to work 1:1 with a patient in order to protect their license and/or so that the patient can claim the fee under their insurance plan
* Professions that require you to lay hands on your patients or clients

The whole point of having a method is so that you avoid working 1:1 with clients and patients whenever possible. But offering an automated method that your ideal clients go through isn't enough to deliver the promised outcome. Remember, if they could get results without you, they would have already. What they're missing is something that they can't get from learning lessons and action tasks, and that's accountability, coaching, and community.

Your signature program should include your method plus additional support components that give you the ability to add in personalization and to provide accountability for your ideal clients. Here are some additional support components that you can add into your signature program to ensure that the program can deliver on its promise.

Weekly or Bi-Weekly Live Office Hours (Group Coaching)

Replace 1:1 calls with a weekly or bi-weekly live group call. This gives your ideal clients the ability to show up, ask questions, get feedback, share challenges and wins, and get coached by you in a group setting. Everyone benefits and you're not repeating yourself.

Facebook Group (Community)

Having a program-specific Facebook group that you refer to as a community is a game-changer for your business. You put all your clients going through your method into the Facebook group. This also cuts off the need for emails as clients are directed to post their questions, etc. in the Facebook group. The biggest benefit of having a group is the ability for your clients to mingle and communicate with each other. They will become real friends and independently create support systems. I am obsessed with my Facebook groups.

Bonuses

Bonuses are additional content that you really want to include in your method, but they're not needed. They're a 'nice to have', not 'need to have'. Creating additional content that helps your ideal client get deeper, faster results and giving it to them for free is a way to overdeliver.

In the next section, I'm going to give you an example of how you can lay out the components of your signature program and deliver it to your ideal client in an automated way that to them feels personalized.

Step 5. Implement Program Delivery

I often receive two contradictory requests. The first: "Lori, would it be possible to get access to all the content now?" The second: "So we're having an issue with the content... there's a number of our clients who feel really overwhelmed because they don't know what to do or where to start. They're wondering if they can get one module at a time, not the whole thing at once."

Both of these scenarios are true stories and happen often. You will never be able to please everyone, and there will always be someone who complains and wants the program delivered another way. We've tested many different ways to deliver program content. In terms of customer satisfaction and client compliance, we've found the easiest delivery method is to give access to the entire program at once. This includes a detailed outline and instructions on how to work through the program content. Then, you send weekly check-in emails with any reminders that are needed.

Sure, you could send out the modules one at a time, but there are many tech tasks and customer service issues that come with doing that. I could spend the next three pages writing about all the reasons why I'd prefer that you give complete program access up front, but that would be a waste. You'll just have to trust that, after working with thousands of clients, I know what I'm talking about. I'll make you a deal. Do it my way first, and then once you understand the tech and how to manage customer service, you can deviate from my recommendation.

Instead of giving you choices for the delivery of your

method and the additional support components, I'm going to outline exactly what we and hundreds of our clients do so you don't have to reinvent the wheel.

Note: To deliver all the program content, you will use your email marketing platform, not a membership site or anything like that. You should revisit the Content Organization section and follow the instructions. You're also going to want to review the terms. You're going to need to do a bit of tech here, and if you're not sure what I'm talking about or how to zip files, you can Google how to do it.

As previously instructed, create a dedicated folder on your desktop and name it Signature Program. Create subfolders for each module, ensuring that each module contains the correct learning lesson and action content (audio, video, PDFs, etc.). Then you will need to zip each module folder. Upload each zipped module folder to a cloud-based platform. Collect the download links for each zipped module. Then, in the signature program access email, you'll list out each module and hyperlink the words "CLICK HERE TO DOWNLOAD MODULE 1" with the download link for Module 1 and so on. This is the path of least resistance.

After you enroll a new client, the process works like this:

Immediate Post Purchase Welcome Email:
- Welcome note
- Outline of the program, including any specific dates to make note of
- Date and time of live office hours (group coaching calls)

- 1:1 call booking instructions (if applicable)
- Link to the Facebook group (if applicable)
- Policies and communication instructions
- Note to watch for email with program links (next steps)

Signature Program Access (send 30 minutes later):
- Welcome paragraph
- Bullet point outline of what's included in the email and things to pay attention to
- Explanation of how to download the program content
- List of modules hyperlinked to the module cloud-based download link
- Instructions on how to communicate if customer service is required
- Reminders of date and time of live office hours (group coaching calls)
- Next steps

Weekly Check-In Email:
- Create one weekly check-in email and send it out weekly
- Do not reference any specific module; instead, provide a motivational or inspirational tip
- Remind about date and time of live office hours (group coaching calls)
- Add in any relevant customer service instructions
- Provide a link to the Facebook group
- Provide next steps

Here's the thing about program delivery. At first, it's a nightmare. There is tech involved, and your ideal clients will have trouble using the computer to access your program, even if they are genius website coders. Some people's browsers won't like the download links, and some people won't even know how to unzip the folders. Some people won't have the ability to listen to your audios or will try to unzip the folder from a smartphone (which you can't do). There are so many things that *will* happen to you. Just know that you're not doing it wrong. Tech breaks. It's unreliable. It's frustrating. You need to learn to take the good with the bad when it comes to running an online business. The good news is that we've never had a program delivery tech issue that Google couldn't solve.

Step 6. Confirm Program Specifics

Now that we've completed the fun stuff, let's move onto the boring, least sexy, but must-include stuff like program policies and legal requirements. The elements that I've included in this section are recommendations. Depending on your designation, scope of practice, and the type of method you offer, you will need to modify the policies and legal recommendations. You will also modify these over time as you gain experience. The policies I've recommended below are to protect you and to give clear guidelines to your ideal client.

Disclaimer: I am not a lawyer. The policies I recommend below do not constitute legal advice. If you are unsure of what legal necessities are required for your designation or you want to protect your business, you must speak to your professional designation certifying body or association and consult with a lawyer.

You are in the health industry, and there are so many gray areas, especially for those of you who want to build your businesses online. Most of the certifying bodies, professional associations, and legislating organizations haven't caught up to running a health or coaching business on the internet. That means it's up to you to do what you can to protect yourself and your clients from harm.

Here is a list of recommended program policies you should create and clearly communicate to your ideal clients:

- Guarantee/refund
- Ongoing access
- Call cancellation/no show for 1:1 calls
- Decline payments
- Office hours/customer service
- Complaints/communication
- Discounts

Guarantee/Refund

- Offer a guarantee that includes a refund if you like, but it's not mandatory.
- Clearly outline the guarantee and refund conditions.
- Clearly outline how to request a refund.
- List the guarantee/refund policy on your terms and conditions page, sales page (if applicable), welcome email, and checkout page (if applicable).

- Specify a timeframe for the refund: after X numbers of days or within X number of days.
- Make it conditional: they have to do XYZ to receive a refund.
- Submit proof to receive a refund—meal plans, logs, survey, etc.

<u>Suggested Wording:</u> If you have completed the first two modules and have submitted XXXX [something actionable that they can complete and submit] within the first 30 days of starting the program and you still aren't happy with the program, then you will receive a full refund.

Ongoing Access

Avoid using the term 'lifetime'; use 'ongoing access' instead. Then decide what specific components of your signature program your clients will have ongoing access to.

- Program content
- Facebook group
- Ongoing coaching
- New bonuses
- Program updates/add-ons

Call Cancellation/No Show for 1:1 Calls

Have these policies clearly stated in your online scheduler reminder-call emails, Facebook group welcome post, and welcome email.

- 24-hour notice to reschedule or cancel

- Policy for multiple reschedules in a row
- Reschedule via online calendar
- No show without explanation
- No show policy
- Forfeit sessions
- Missed group sessions

Decline Payments

Decline payments will occur when you offer a payment plan. You must review your daily sales to ensure you don't miss decline payments.

Templated email decline sequence

- Email #1: sent immediately upon decline with a three-day deadline
- Email #2: three days later: bring account up to date within the next two business days or the client will be withdrawn from the program until the account is brought up to date
- Email #3: two days after the previous: notice of interruption until the account is brought up to date
- Email #4: one day after the previous: service has been interrupted and will remain interrupted until the account has been brought up to date
- Continued emails on a weekly basis (include phone calls if phone number is available)
- Remove all applicable program access

Office Hours/Customer Service

- Have a dedicated email for customer service.
- Use a customer service autoresponder outlining support hours and email response time. Do not respond outside that window.
- Add these policies to your Facebook welcome post and description.
- Create and stick to the boundaries.

Complaints/Communication

- Address the comments and complaints that matter. Client complaints will happen.
- Handle mistakes quickly with personal responsibility.
- Have a feedback form where complaints can be submitted.
- Address concerns quickly without defensiveness.

Discounts

- If you offer a special bonus or discount, will you still give them the offer if they miss the deadline? Your choice.
- Do you provide special offers for friends and family?

Legal Requirements

Again, I am not a lawyer. Here is a list of some legal requirements:

- Medical Disclaimer

- Insurance
- Privacy Policy (essential for advertising on the internet)
- Terms and Conditions (not a legal requirement but highly recommended)

There are many great templates for all these requirements on the internet. Do a Google search. Visit websites for businesses that offer similar programs and services.

Before we dive into the components of each of these, I want to address the issue of protecting your content. One of the most common questions I get is, "How do I prevent people from sharing my content or giving their friends access to my paid program?"

Here's the thing... you can't really prevent this.

You need to make your download links public, and you need to give your clients access to their content via emails (these can easily be forwarded). Even if you're using a membership site to deliver your program content, the person can share their username and password with friends. It will happen so there's no sense in wasting energy trying to stop it. This is the reason that making your additional support elements (accountability, support, and community) an essential part of the program is so important. You can control access to these.

The best method to avoid the sharing of your program is to address it in your terms and conditions under a single user license (Google this).

Medical Disclaimer

A medical disclaimer is a statement that provides the intent of the information so that it's not to be confused with medical advice. A medical disclaimer defines the author's responsibility and therefore reduces the risk of harm. Having one protects you so it doesn't matter what designation you have or whether your profession is regulated.

You should include a medical disclaimer on the terms and conditions section of your website. Anything you create that is not directly on your website (including free material and paid program content) should also include a medical disclaimer.

Insurance

You should acquire professional liability insurance of at least $1 million. Make sure your professional coverage is adequate for all your different designations—more than one type of insurance may be required if you have more than one designation. For example, if you're both a yoga instructor and a health coach, you may need two types of insurance. You should include coverage for enhancements, for example, food demos and supplement recommendations. Include international web-based insurance (virtual coaching and online programs) if applicable. Ensure you have office protection, if needed. For example, you may require coverage if you're traveling with equipment. Include tenant's insurance if you work out of a clinic or clients' homes.

Privacy Policy

A privacy policy is a statement that discloses some or all of the ways you as a business entity gather, use, disclose, and manage a customer's or client's data. It fulfills a *legal* requirement to protect a customer's or client's privacy.

A privacy policy is a legal requirement if you are going to be collecting anyone's personal information, which you will be doing.

Terms and Conditions

A terms and conditions page is the web page that sets out the rules for your business, website, and online brand. It sits beside your privacy policy page and outlines your terms and conditions. It's not a legal requirement like the privacy policy, but you should still have one.

Are you still awake? I hope so, because the next section is where you start to collect feedback on your program from real human beings.

Step 7. Collect Feedback and Iterate.

"How do I know if this is going to work? What if nobody gets results? Am I giving them too much information? What if I'm not giving them enough? What if I move this module around and add in that action task? Should I scrap the whole thing and just start over?"

These are some of the questions I get from clients after they have finished creating and recording their content. Fear sets in, and it's like they're stuck in a state of asking, "What if it's not good enough?" Their first instinct is to edit their program, even though they have no evidence that it won't work. So they spend the next three to six months fixing it... even though they have no idea where it's broken.

There's a big reason why you feel unsure about your program: no proof of concept.

You've created a method based on your own experience and on research and scientific evidence, but you haven't tested it yet. So, it only makes sense that you're nervous it's going to suck. The way to get over that fear and build up some proof and gain confidence is to test out the program, get feedback from clients, and have the ability to make any improvements before you scale it.

Why Is Collecting Feedback Important?

You've put together an educated guess in the form of a method, and now you've got to test it with clients to determine to what degree your hypothesis is correct. I've never heard of a hypothesis proven perfect on the first try.

In other words, just because you've done the work to finish your program doesn't mean that it's 100% perfect. It's not. There's no way it could be. The only way to know where and how to improve it so that you can feel confident about delivering the promised outcome in a repeatable way is by putting ideal clients through the program and collecting their feedback. Instruct them to give you honest, constructive feedback—what's too confusing, what's too hard, where there's not enough information, where more or less support is needed, and so on.

Here's something I want you to keep at the top of your mind as you go through this process. You are no longer your ideal client, and while you might think that your program is amazing (and I'm sure it is), you have a level of understanding ten times past that of your ideal client, so you're not going to be able to gauge with any level of certainty if your ideal clients can actually comply with your action tasks. And if they can't comply with even 50% of what you're asking them to do, then they won't get the results you've promised them. This is why I strongly recommend that you collect feedback before scaling your program. You need to work out the kinks first.

The truth is, you will likely have to iterate your program several times before it's at a place where you feel really good about it and where clients can easily go through it with minimal questions and achieve consistent results.

When that happens, you'll use the program as is for a year or two, and then because you've gained so much experience and wisdom, you're going to want to redo it from scratch, which is totally normal. I've redone each of my signature programs at least five times, and I continue to adjust and make improvements as needed, based on client results and feedback.

How to Collect Feedback

Feedback. It's important that you are explicit about your feedback expectations. Your clients should be able to give you feedback in a structured way. Asking for feedback won't necessarily yield quality feedback. Be clear about the type, amount, and frequency of feedback that your clients should provide. You could have an agenda or an outline that provides specific instructions on when and how to provide feedback.

It's also important that you put your ego aside and openly receive feedback. The more feedback you get, the easier it will be to improve your program and the client's experience.

It might happen that you get a lot of feedback, which to you means that your program isn't good. With all due respect, that might be true—this is the first time you've put a signature program together. That is why you collect feedback, so you can understand what's not working and make it better before opening it up to the wider public. Give yourself some grace... this is all new to you. The first time you do anything it's rarely awesome.

Iterating the Content. I highly recommend that you wait until your clients finish the program before you start making changes to the content. You're going to want to dive right into making changes after every piece of feedback you receive. Show restraint. Wait until you have all the feedback so that you can go through a review process and then make any changes.

MIA Clients. Not all clients will finish the program, even though they committed to it. Some clients will communicate with you, and others will simply go missing in action. That's okay. That has nothing to do with you. They are embarrassed. Continue to follow up with kindness. Focus on getting feedback from the clients who are present and continuing with your program.

Take a Breath

Holy crap! You've come so far. Do me a favor. Before I put all this together and tie a bow around it for you, I want you to do something for me. It might feel silly but just do it, okay?

Get into a comfortable position. Close your eyes. Take some deep breaths. Fill your belly with air and exhale. Keeping your eyes closed, I want you to smile. Like, a big smile, and continue smiling. In your mind (or out loud if you have the courage), I want you to say this:

"[say your name], I am so proud of you. [Say your name], you've done it. You've created your method and you've collected feedback. Congratulations."

It's no one else's job to feel proud of you. No one else needs to give you a pat on the back and tell you that you're doing a good job. Just like it's no one else's job to be disappointed in you if things don't work out on the first attempt. It's your job to feel proud of yourself and to be able to recognize and celebrate when you've made progress. The whole 'saying your name to yourself' thing is a wonderful trick I learned from Brendon Burchard. It feels weird at first, but it totally works.

We often look for external validation and recognition, and when it doesn't come as expected, we let that invalidate our hard focus and progress. Not anymore. This trick of using your own name and repeating to yourself what you want to hear tricks your brain and helps you actually feel the way you want to feel—as though someone else is saying it to you.

Because it's no one else's job to make you feel the way you want to feel. And the best thing is, you can use this trick anytime you need it.

Step 8. Put It All Together

"It's nice to meet you, Lori. What do you do?"

"Me? Oh. Um. I'm a registered holistic nutritionist."

"That's nice."

She was my ideal client. I was at a fundraiser event that my mom had organized. My mom and her friends were *all* my ideal clients, and I was messing up my opportunity to open up the conversation with them because I was the worst at self-promoting. The absolute worst! I didn't know how to talk about what I did in a way that would invite curiosity and open up the conversation that could lead to scheduling a sales call.

I think back to so many missed opportunities—most of them from talking to complete strangers at the grocery store. When someone would ask me what I did, I would respond with my professional title, thinking that my profession was enough for them to want to know more.

Nope. Not the case. Instead, my response should have been my pitch (and it was, after I caught on)…

"What do I do? Well, I work with menopausal women who can't seem to lose weight despite trying all the diets. I get them to lose weight without having to give up wine, chocolate, or popcorn."

As soon as I switched to this response, I almost always got the following in return: "How? I need your help." Even when I wasn't talking with my ideal client, whoever I was talking with would ask, "I'm not menopausal but can you help me?" It even happened with men! They'd ask for help but feel the need to let me know they weren't menopausal. Yeah, thanks, Captain Obvious.

Now that you have a method and have decided what additional support you're going to include to create your signature program package, let's focus on how you're going to talk about your signature program so that the next time you are at the grocery store or a party, you take advantage of any opportunities that present themselves.

I'm going to give you a template so that you can clearly and confidently talk about what you do in a way that provokes curiosity and elicits the only desirable response: "I need your help." Of course, if you're not talking with a potential ideal client and don't really want to engage in conversation, then just tell them your professional designation and that should shut them down immediately.

In order to have a clear and concise elevator pitch, you need to have clarity around the following, which you should already have at this point:

- Who do you help?
- The problem your program solves (as your ideal client experiences it)
- The outcome your program gets for your ideal clients
- Something they want to gain or things they don't want to give up

Then just fill in the blank spots using the template:

"I work with [who do you help] who struggle with [problem according to the ideal client]. I get them to [outcome they want] so they can [hopes/dreams]."

Or,

"I work with [who do you help] who struggle with [problem according to the ideal client]. I get them to [outcome they want] without [things they don't want to give up]."

That's it. That's how you talk about your business the next time someone asks you what you do. You use that template. You don't launch into a whole explanation of your professional designation, the modules, the Facebook group, etc. Brevity is the name of the game. You want the person you're talking with to be curious so that they ask you questions, versus you vomiting all the things you can down their throat.

You are a practitioner or coach with expertise in a specific niche, a signature method that gets your clients results, and a program that gives you the ability to work with ideal clients from all over the world.

This is who you are now. This is your business.

The last pillar of the Health Expert Business Model is important, and it comes last for a very specific reason. Pillar 5: Keep Clients for Life deals with what happens next. After your ideal client is done working with you in your signature program, even if they didn't finish the program, show up, or get the full outcome they desired, they're going to ask you, "What's next? How do I continue to work with you?" This is where they ascend to your next program so that you can do exactly that.

Action Steps

→ Give yourself six to eight weeks to work through the eight steps to create your method and signature program.

→ Collect feedback and iterate.

→ Avoid overthinking and overanalyzing your program.

Chapter 10

Pillar 5:
KEEP CLIENTS FOR LIFE

"*Working* with you has changed my life. All I wanted was to lose 23lb. What I got was my life back. I didn't realize how miserable I was. I didn't realize how much I shrunk when I walked into a room. I no longer do that. I stand up tall. You helped me to do that. But what do I do now? How do I continue to work with you? Our time is done."

I've kept Diane's email ever since she sent it to me on November 23, 2012. Diane was a smart, savvy, and well-dressed woman. I reference her style because I have none, and I always admired how poised and polished she was. Her husband was a very successful lawyer, and she was done feeling ashamed about her weight.

I looked forward to my sessions with her because she genuinely wanted to work through her shit and lose the weight. So when I got that email, I cried. I cried because there were clients who followed my recommendations and never lost the weight. Then there were clients who genuinely had a transformation and would likely never regain the weight. I knew she would be one of the latter. But I didn't know how we could continue to work together aside from renewing her for another round of the WOW! Weight Loss program. So I did what I always did (and still do)—I made it up.

At that point, the WOW! Weight Loss program was running in five gyms, and I had my office in a medical doctor's practice. I had three prominent doctors referring their patients to me any time there were weight-related blood test result abnormalities, before medications were prescribed.

I couldn't see back then that we all have levels of healing that we journey through. Your signature program, just like the WOW! Weight Loss program, is the baseline level of healing. It's the fundamentals. Even if that first level is only completed at 25 or 50%, it's our natural inclination to want to move on to the next level. This is where Pillar 5: Keep Clients for Life comes into play.

There are two scenarios that you'll encounter when working with clients:

Scenario # 1: Redo the signature program.

Scenario # 2: Ascend them to the next level.

There will be a certain percentage of clients who should redo your signature program because they haven't yet implemented enough of the recommended action tasks to get the desired outcome. In this case, moving them to the next-level program isn't in their best interests. You don't want to put the cart before the horse. If a client isn't drinking water, eating the way you need them to, or following your recommendations consistently at least 50% of the time, it's not going to be helpful for them to move to a program where you take them deeper and ask more of them. This is where you would recommend that they redo your signature program. On the other hand, there will be a percentage of clients who are ready for a deeper level of healing. If you decide that they are ready, based on your professional assessment, then you would enroll them into your next-level program.

To grow your business, get clients, and ditch your day job, you only need one signature program. But if you want to be the kind of practitioner or coach who supports your clients throughout their healing journey, then you can add on a next-level program. As your client base graduates to the next level, you can continue to add programs that support them.

When we work with clients who are at the beginning stages of building their business, they inevitably start to ask, "What's next?" My answer is always the same: build your audience, learn how to turn ideal prospects into ideal clients, focus on getting your signature program running, focus on getting your current clients consistent results, and then pay attention to what your clients need from you in order to get the next-level result. Sure, you can brainstorm ideas for your next-level program now, but I promise you that whatever you come up with will change once you start working with clients.

Here's why I don't recommend building two programs—your signature program (which offers the fundamentals) and your next-level program (which offers a deeper level of healing)—at the same time.

Reason # 1: They Are Different Ideal Clients.

Remember back to the +1 Pillar: Who Do You Want to Serve?, where I had you define your ideal client profile. Yes, it's the same person, but their problem isn't the same anymore. Because they've worked with you for a period of time, they now have a new, next-level set of problems that will require a new method to fix.

Reason # 2: You Don't Know What They Need.

If you haven't had much client experience yet, then it's reasonable to assume that you don't know what those next-level clients will need. So it's a waste of time to start creating the next-level program before the first one is successful. Does that make sense?

Reason # 3: You Will Need a Stronger Business Infrastructure.

In order to help your ideal clients with their new problem, you'll have to create a new method, which will require your time, energy, and attention. If your first method isn't running like a machine, then you'll likely end up doing a poor job with both programs.

I want you to focus on growing your business and getting clients so you can quit your day job. Running two programs at once requires a stronger business infrastructure because it means two sales offers, two client groups with different needs, way more customer service, and more of your time, energy, and attention. I want you to first build a solid business foundation to grow from before you take on more.

The 'next-level' program isn't the same thing as offering 1:1 sessions as an add-on to your signature program.

Having a next-level program requires the creation of an entirely new program that your signature program clients ascend into if and when they are ready to continue their healing journey.

Two examples of next-level programs:

- A maintenance program where you provide ongoing support and accountability.
- A longer-term, higher-priced signature program that delivers a next-level method for them to follow.

As someone who has built a multimillion-dollar business that offers different levels of programs for clients based on the stages that they're at, my advice to you would be to give yourself time to create and implement one program at a time. Yes, I'm planting the seed so you know what's next for you, but before you build the second floor of your house, you should make sure that your foundation can support that growth.

There was a point in my business-building journey where I had to put the brakes on because my internal infrastructure couldn't support adding more. I was tapped out. There were no more hours in the day. My house was full, so to speak. What that meant for me was that I had to renovate my house. I had to rebuild my infrastructure so that I could support the growth of the business. I had to build and train a team to help me before I could take on more; otherwise I'd just add on more—more clients, more programs—and my house would implode.

You will create and add on additional programs when you're ready. Don't give into the pressure that makes you feel like you need to have more than one signature program when you're in the building stage, which, if you're reading this, is probably the stage that you're in. Focus on building the best possible initial signature program that you can which will get results for your clients, and when you and your business feel like you're ready to expand, then you can add on more.

I used the WOW! Weight Loss program as my only program and built a multi-six-figure business. So if I can do it, you can too!

Action Steps

→ Brainstorm next-level programs.

→ Focus on creating and implementing your signature program first before you create your next one.

Chapter 11

WILL THIS WORK FOR ME?

I tried to squeeze myself into the desk/chair combo at the back of the room, hoping that nobody would notice that an obviously pregnant person was taking the exercise physiology class. I bet the other people in the class thought, "Wow, a pregnant university student! Good luck." Except I was 28 years old and about to have my second child!

In 2010, even though the WOW! Weight Loss program was in all four of the gym's locations and I was doing well—making money, paying the bills, and even having a little bit left over—I was still unconvinced that I was going to be successful. Granted, I hadn't defined what successful actually meant to me yet, but I just wasn't feeling it. I didn't feel secure. Looking back, maybe it was because my marriage was about to implode… But hey, hindsight is 20/20.

Self-doubt kicked in hard. What if the gym cancels my program? Then what am I going to do? What if the new nutritionist I hire to take over the program screws it all up? What if I get fired? What if I don't want to go back to work? What if I can't go back to work? For months, my mind was spinning out of control with all the 'what if' thoughts. So I did what any normal pregnant person does. I decided to go back to school to become a teacher. In order for me to become a physical education teacher, I had to take three additional university classes.

No problem. I've got this. Full-time business. A two-and-a-half-year-old, and I'm pregnant. Yup, totally sane decision on my part. My body does not like being pregnant, and so even at four months I looked and felt like I was about six months—so you can imagine what it was like to fit into that chair with the writing desk attached: wasn't going to happen.

I finished those classes and did quite well, considering I had pregnancy brain. I was proud of myself. I had a fallback plan. Becoming a teacher sounded like a secure, good gig. It felt safe. And at that point I was craving safety and security.

I wanted someone to guarantee that I would become successful, that my nutrition practice would grow, and that it would all be okay. I wanted confirmation that at some point, sooner rather than later, I'd feel legit—like I knew what I was doing, and that all the hard work would be worthwhile. I was looking for a type of security that didn't exist on the career path I had chosen, although I didn't know that then. And so the whole teacher idea.

Daniel was born in March of 2011. By April of 2011 my marriage was over and in May of 2011, I had what I now call my No Plan B Decision. I was sitting on my king-size bed with my two babies in the first house I had ever owned, thinking, "okay, I've got to figure this out. I am on my own now." I had already decided there was no way I was going to take alimony. I would only take child support. It was up to me to provide for myself.

Being a teacher was no longer an option for me because I couldn't go back to school full-time. I had to work. I had two little mouths to feed.

At that moment, I decided that I was going to figure it out. I decided that I was going to dramatically change my life. I decided that I was going to be financially independent and build a business that gave me the ability to be with my kids and still work. I decided that I was going to become more successful than I had ever dreamed possible and that I would be able to take care of myself and my two kids without ever having to rely on anyone else for financial support.

I made a decision to go all in. No matter what. Even though I didn't feel ready. I also felt like I didn't have a choice.

The only problem was that I had no idea how I was going to transform my life. I had no idea what I needed to do to become successful. I had no idea how I was going to further grow my business. I had no examples of what 'more success' looked like.

So I wrote all my desires in my journal.

I journaled about the kind of life I wanted for myself and how I wanted it to look and feel. I asked God for answers. I promised that I would do whatever it took for as long as it was going to take, as long as I was able to remain financially independent and in complete control of my time so I could be around for my babies. I asked for answers every single day.

Then I started to Google. But in 2011, it wasn't today's

Google. It was probably Yahoo or something like that. I distinctly remember searching "how to make more money as a nutritionist." I found these two guys, Bedros and Craig. They were teaching personal trainers how to build six-figure businesses using digital products and selling them online. I started to read their blogs. What they were saying made sense. I was hooked. This was my answer. Thank you, God. Yes, I could take my nutrition business online. Easy-peasy... LOL.

In this book I've given you everything I wish I had known when I was starting to grow my nutrition practice and taking my business online. But I know that having this book (and me) in your corner—reassuring you a thousand times over that all you have to do is follow what I have outlined and you'll grow your business, get clients, and be able to quit your day job—isn't enough to get you to take action. Having the proven steps, strategies, tactics, and even proof that it's worked for other people isn't enough when the question *'will this work for me?'* is playing on repeat in your mind. So let's address it head on so that we can quiet that voice—so you can take imperfect action and make progress toward turning your vision (that you already created) into a reality.

I asked my community specifically for feedback so that I could make sure I got this part right. I asked:

What Is Stopping You from Taking Action?

In less than six hours, I got 53 comments. I'm going to summarize the responses so that you can see that you are not alone in having these feelings. I can give you all the answers about why and how the Health Expert Business Model will work for you. I can show you thousands of practitioners and coaches who have created their own signature programs and are working with clients. I can show you examples of my clients who started with zero business experience and within two years are making six figures. I started online in 2012 and now have a multimillion-dollar company, a team of 16 amazing people, and a community of tens of thousands; in addition, I am 100% financially independent. But none of this proof matters if Resistance and fear are blocking you from stepping into and owning your Power.

So if you have that annoying voice in your head asking on repeat, "Will this work for me?" take a look at some of the comments below and pick the ones that resonate with you the most. It's important for you to be able to identify the false belief (the lie) that is preventing you from moving forward or even getting started.

Once you identify the lie, there's no going back. Either you choose to do the work to dismantle the lie, or you choose to keep on believing it and never make any progress at all.

Here are some of those responses.

FEAR OF FAILURE: What if I'm not good enough? What if I don't know enough? What if I can't get results for my clients? What if nobody buys? What if I can't make it work? What if I work so hard for so long and nothing happens? What if people pay me, and I don't get them results? There are so many other practitioners and coaches out there; why would someone work with me?

IMPOSTER SYNDROME: I feel like a fraud. I'm experiencing self-doubt. I feel inadequate. I don't know what I'm doing, but I know I'm supposed to project confidence and certainty. I don't want to put myself out there. I don't have enough experience. Who am I to be doing this? I'm afraid that people will find out that I don't have what it takes.

STILL ON A HEALTH JOURNEY: I need to lose weight before I can work with clients. I'm still trying to heal myself. I still struggle with my own health. I don't want to burn out. I have flare-ups. I'm not sure I want to share what's going on with my own health.

FEAR OF JUDGMENT: I'm afraid to put myself out there because of what other people will think. I'm afraid that I'm going to piss people off. I'm scared of what my family, friends, and work colleagues will think. I'm afraid of criticism, trolls, and negative comments.

FEAR OF SUCCESS: I'm afraid to step into my own power and own my awesomeness. I'm afraid to take a risk because if it works out, then how will I handle it all? What if I'm not able to handle the pressure? If I make more money than my spouse, I worry that it will negatively impact our relationship. If I make more money than anyone else in my family, I'm afraid that I will appear ostentatious. I worry that I'll be successful and then it will all implode. It's really scary to reach for more. It's really uncomfortable to take the road less traveled.

The question 'will it work for me?' is a cover-up for what's really going on. I've been doing my own work to process through my limiting beliefs for years and have worked with thousands of practitioners and coaches to know that 'will it work for me?' isn't really the question. Even if I showed you exactly how the Health Expert Business Model would work for you, you would still have underlying beliefs that have the power to stop you at every single stage of development.

Will the Health Expert Business Model work for you, specifically? Yes, 100%. And I don't even need to know anything about you to confidently say that. I have a decade of proof behind me, thousands of clients, and real success stories backing up my answer. It doesn't matter what professional designation you have, whether you have client experience or not, what your niche is, or where you live. It doesn't matter what your age is. It doesn't matter how many kids you have or don't have. It doesn't matter whether your spouse, family, loved ones, or colleagues are supportive or not. None of those things matter... the Health Expert Business Model works.

The only reason why it won't work is because you've *chosen* to fight for your limitations. And you know what happens when you fight hard for your limitations, right? You get to keep them.

I realized very quickly that if I wanted to transform my life and grow a business that truly had an impact on the world, then I would need to become very comfortable with being uncomfortable. I would have to become friends with my fear and be okay taking big risks without any assurance that they would pay off. I had to double down on my self-belief, tenacity, and ability to get back up after I've been knocked down.

As Oprah would say, *"We can't become who we need to be by remaining who we are."* I knew that in order for me to get what I wanted, I would need to change—my habits, my mindset, my work ethic, and my discipline. And only then would this whole thing work.

I know it sounds a bit Pollyanna or pie in the sky to say that in order to grow your business, get clients, and ditch your day job, you've got to overcome your limiting beliefs, because self-sabotage is a powerful force. But until you have overcome them, you will continue to feel like you're working so hard without making any progress.

Because no amount of strategy, tactics, coaching, or mentorship will work until you decide to step into your power and claim success despite being afraid. Those practitioners and coaches who feel the fear and do it anyway, those are the ones you should be comparing yourself with because they are the ones who get it. It's working for them because they've chosen to acknowledge all the feelings and do it anyway.

You want to make it work? How badly?

You want to grow your business, get clients, and finally ditch your day job or contribute to your household? You want to be able to buy things without a second thought, spend hundreds of dollars a month on supplements and organic food, go on luxury vacations, have a cleaning service, send your kids to overnight camp for the whole summer, get out of debt, pay off your mortgage, buy a cottage, travel whenever you want?...

Who do you have to become in order to make these things happen?

Are you ready to make your No Plan B Decision and commit to following through, even though you're afraid and uncertain, because you know that's the only way to make it really work?

I believe that you have what it takes. I believe that you are courageous and brave and that you will have a massive impact in your corner of the world. I believe that you are afraid and feel unsure of yourself. I know that those feelings never really go away. I know that the hard work, sacrifice, and struggle are put there as a test to separate the leaders from the followers. Choose to be a leader. Choose, every single day, to show up for the strangers searching for you on the internet, for your clients, for your family, and most importantly, for yourself.

Chapter 12

BUILD THE BUSINESS AND LIFE OF YOUR DREAMS

I was standing in High Park (a beautiful spot in downtown Toronto) with a film crew, ready to film a video series to promote a program we were about to launch. It was the perfect day. The sun was shining, but in the right direction so it didn't mess up our shot. It was warm. The flowers were in full bloom. And my hair and makeup were on point, which is always important. I was ready.

It's possible that you've seen the photo of me in a blue shirt smiling into a big white flower. I love that shot. To me that photo represents 'possibility'. That day was the first time I said my mantra out loud. It's the day I claimed #mylifemyterms, and I haven't looked back since.

That day was the first time I taught the Health Expert Business Model. It was the first time I shared the process that helped me to build the business and life of my dreams, all on my own terms. In this book I taught you the same framework that I taught back in 2014. I'm just way better at teaching it now.

My intention in writing this book was to give you two things...

The first was to give you a proven model that walks you through, step-by-step, how to set up your business and have a solid foundation to grow from so that you can stand out from the crowd, get clients, and ditch your day job. Now that you've read this book you know The Health Expert Business Model. You've walked hand in hand with me through the steps and have the knowledge to do the following:

- Create a vision for your business and life and a mission for your business so that you have a final destination to work toward.
- Pillar +1: Who Do You Want to Serve? gave you the framework to define who you want to work with so you can have the impact you desire in your corner of the world.
- Pillar 1: How to Stand Out from the Crowd taught you how to stand out from the crowd and use content to attract your ideal clients so that they know that you and your solution to their problem exists.
- Pillar 2: The KLT + E Sequence gave you the ability to nurture and engage with your audience and get them to know, trust, and like you before you ask them to work with you.
- Pillar 3: Getting the YES! enabled you to create a structured sales process so that you could turn your ideal prospect into your ideal client in the least salesy way possible.

- Pillar 4: Build the Methodology (The Signature Program) outlined how you're going to work with clients and get them results in a way that allows you to scale your business.
- Pillar 5: Keep Clients for Life planted the seed for what's next so that you can create more programs that fully support your ideal clients through their healing journey.

But merely reading this book won't do you any good. If reading a book about how to grow a business, get clients, and ditch your day job was all it took, there wouldn't be any broke practitioners and coaches. But there are. There are a lot of them, sadly. And that's because they lack the other thing I intended to give you by writing this book.

The second thing is the belief that the ideas and the dreams you have for your future are valid and attainable. My wish for you is that you now believe that by using The Health Expert Business Model it is absolutely possible for you to build the business and life of your dreams, no matter where you're starting from or what your circumstances are. Those broke practitioners failed to do two things that set those who are successful apart from those who stay stuck: 1) take imperfect action every day, even when you don't feel like you know what you're doing, and 2) believe in yourself like it's your job.

Before I sign off, it is my hope that by sharing my story with you and the exact framework that took me from being a preachy, naive, unskilled, broke registered holistic nutritionist to a CEO who now runs a global multimillion-dollar business from her dining room table, you now feel empowered, motivated, and, more importantly, capable of following through.

Whatever impact you desire to have—whether it's to give burnt-out moms their energy back; to help menopausal women lose weight; to give parents the tools to support their ADHD children; to help people overcome anxiety; to get rid of back pain; to help people get rid of gas or bloating; or simply to help people sleep through the night—whatever your mission is, I hope that you decide to make your No Plan B Decision. I believe in your courage to quiet the voices in your mind, to ignore the well-meaning but passive-aggressive family members telling you that your dreams are silly and that quitting your cushy corporate job is a mistake, and to give yourself permission to fully go for it.

Do not deny yourself the opportunity to build a business that could transform lives because you're afraid that it won't work or because someone else doesn't believe in you or because you won't be perfect at it. Who does that serve? No one. The people who desperately need and want your help are out there, and they are actively searching for you right now. That feeling you have in the pit of your stomach isn't fear, it's purpose. It's purpose that got you to pick up this book in the first place because I know that you were put on this earth to transform lives—both your own, and the lives of your clients.

It's time to honor that purpose, take yourself seriously, and believe with every fiber of your being that it's possible for you. You deserve to have the business and life of your dreams, without apology.

I believe in you.

ACKNOWLEDGMENTS

First and foremost, I have to thank you, my community and my clients. I dedicated this book to you because without you, I wouldn't get to do this work that fulfils me so completely, even on the darkest days. When I offered my very first workshop to teach the pillars in this book—three months postpartum and a hot, leaky, and sweaty mess—you paid me money and showed up. When I threw together my first live event, you bought tickets. When I launched my first online program on December 26, your purchases helped me pay my bills. When I got divorced and finally shared about it, you sent me the most supportive and loving notes.

When I made my first million dollars we celebrated. When I launched the Business of Becoming podcast, you listened and still listen. When I told you I was writing a book, your response was, "Well, it's about time!"

Now together as a community made up of tens of thousands of practitioners and coaches from all over the world, we're measurably changing the way the alternative health and coaching industry operates so that there's way fewer broke and burnt-out professionals and way more clients getting better.

And none of this would be possible without my amazing team of unicorns who work mostly behind the scenes to take my vision, my nonstop ideas, and my relentless pursuit of growth and turn them into a reality. We are most certainly creating opportunities for us to live our best lives, and I'm so grateful that we get to do it together.

Over the years, I've had the pleasure of working with many contractors, most of whom I've never met or even had a live conversation with, and some who have been working for me for years. You've filled in the very large gaps with your skills and expertise. You supported me, and I'm so thankful that we got to work together.

Thank you to Bryan, the father of my children, the person with whom I co-parent, for never telling me to stop working so hard. I am who I've become in large part because of our journey, and I am grateful for that.

To my parents, grandparents, and family… there are no words. Thank you doesn't seem powerful enough. I've never been afraid to just go for it because you've been in my corner the whole time.

And lastly, to the two people who have chosen me to be their mom, Alexis and Daniel. Being your mom is the absolute greatest honor of my life. You are my greatest teachers, and I am eternally grateful that I get to do life with you. I love you both.

ABOUT THE AUTHOR

Lori Kennedy is a former registered holistic nutritionist and the host of the Business of Becoming podcast. She's the founder and CEO of The Wellness Business Hub, an online platform that arms alternative health practitioners and coaches with the business knowledge, actionable strategies, and personal development training needed to grow impactful and thriving online businesses.

As a mom who grew her multimillion-dollar company from her dining room table, she's empowering her community to think outside the box to build the business and life of their dreams, all on their own terms.

You can find her on Instagram @lorikennedyinc or join her online community on Facebook by searching Take Your Health Practice Online.

A RESOURCE YOU WANT & NEED

If you haven't guessed by now, I'm all about taking imperfect action, and the best place to start is by picking your niche and deciding who you want to work with the most. Even if you have your niche and ideal client, further refining is always recommended. In my experience, Pillar +1: Who Do You Want to Serve? (Nail This or Risk Failing) is also the pillar that stalls most practitioners and coaches from gaining momentum.

To help you pick your niche (and define your ideal client), I've created an exclusive masterclass that you can access 100 percent free by visiting **THEWBH.COM/BOOKMASTERCLASS**. In this 45-minute, video-based masterclass, I'm going to walk you through the most profitable niches in the health and coaching industry and help you decide on which niche to pick as a starting point. You'll also get a bonus cheat sheet that will help you stand out from the crowd regardless of the niche you choose.

Head over to **THEWBH.COM/BOOKMASTERCLASS** now to get access.

Printed in Poland
by Amazon Fulfillment
Poland Sp. z o.o., Wrocław